CW00411148

ONLY PROSTITUTES
MARRY IN MAY

Drama Series 9

DACIA MARAINI

ONLY PROSTITUTES
MARRY IN MAY

FOUR PLAYS

EDITED AND WITH AN INTRODUCTION
BY RHODA HELFMAN KAUFMAN

GUERNICA
TORONTO•BUFFALO•LANCASTER (U.K.)
1998

Application for performing rights of these plays
should be addressed to
Avv. Giovanna Cav, Cav-Moradi-Magnosi,
via Maria Adelaide, 8, 00196 Roma, Italia.
Originally published in 1994.

Antonio D'Alfonso, editor
Guernica Editions Inc.
P.O. Box 117, Station P, Toronto (ON), Canada M5S 2S6
250 Sonwil Drive, Buffalo, N.Y. 14225-5516 U.S.A.
Gazelle, Falcon House, Queen Square, Lancaster LA1 1RN U.K.
Printed in Canada.

Legal Deposit — First Quarter
National Library of Canada
Library of Congress Card Number: 93-77802.
Canadian Cataloguing in Publication Data
Maraini, Dacia
Only prostitutes marry in May
(Drama series ; 9)
Translated from Italian.
ISBN 0-920717-81-0
I. Title. II. Series.
PQ4873.A69065   1998   852'.914   C93-090112-6

Table of Contents

TO KAREN AND JENNIFER

'... so that you will remember that ties between women are the strongest and most lasting ...'

INTRODUCTION

Introduction

Dacia Maraini's Background and Literary Works

Dacia Maraini comes from a writing family. Her father, a well-known anthropologist, has written books about Tibet and Japan. Her father's mother, born Polish but naturalized Irish, wrote travel books in English. Maraini's paternal grandfather was a sculptor who lived in Florence and wrote about art and esthetics. Her maternal grandfather was a Sicilian who wrote philosophy. He also published a vegetarian cookbook in 1912.

During her youth, Maraini's family lived in Japan for eight years. Two of those years were spent in an internment camp because of her father's anti-fascist activities. After finishing her studies in Sicily she went to Rome, where she began to get her writings published. There she also met Alberto Moravia and Pier Paolo Pasolini. In 1963, she received the Prix Formentor, an international award, for her novel *L'Eta del malessere (Age of Discontent)*. That novel has since been translated into twelve languages.

Maraini has written ten other novels, including *A memoria (By Heart)*, 1967; *Memoria di una ladra (Memories of a Lady Thief)*, 1973; *Donna in guerra (Woman At War)*, 1975; *Lettere a Marina (Letters to Marina)*, 1981; and *Isolina*, 1985. Her most recent novel, *La lunga vita di Marianna Ucria (The Long Life of Marianna Ucria)*, 1990, was awarded the 1991 Premio Campiello, widely regarded as Italy's equivalent of the Pulitzer Prize. Her book of short stories, *Mio Marito (My Husband)*, was published in 1968.

She has also written both criticism and plays for the theatre. Her works published in Italian include: *Il Ricatto à teatro e altre commédie* (1970), *I sogni di Clitennestra e altre commédie* (1981), *Lezioni d'amore* (1982), and *Stravaganze* (1987). Four published books of poems are: *Crudeltà all'aria aperta* (1968), *Donne mie* (1974), *Mangiami pure* (1979), and *Dimenticato di dimenticare* (1982).

In 1980, Maraini wrote *Storia di Piera*, in collaboration with Piera Degli Esposti. It was made into a film by Marco Ferreri. In 1986 her interviews with Alberto Moravia, *Il bambino Alberto*, were published.

In all, Maraini has written more than thirty plays, at least ten of which have been performed outside Italy. Five were performed in Australia through the efforts of Tony Mitchell, who has translated several of her plays. As her work has become more widely known to American and Canadian audiences, there has been a growing demand for her plays.

This book is the first publication of plays by Maraini in English.

Her Themes

Maraini's writing has touched on many themes. However, several recur and seem to me central to her concerns as a writer and a woman.

First and foremost is the theme of desire, sensuality, and eroticism as important and legitimate dimensions of women's lives. Maraini repeatedly affirms the importance of the body, and women's natural closeness to their bodies. She also probes deeply into hidden erotic feelings, especially the incestual yearning for the parent's body, the desire to reconnect with one's mother or father. She has often quoted Roland Barthes' saying that writing itself is 'like playing with the body of your mother.'

For Maraini, writing is a sensual experience: tasting the words, feeling the rhythm of the language. The subject of her writing is itself an exploration of sensuality, especially of sexuality. Not merely sexual experience or sexual politics, but the entire, rich spectrum of personal, spiritual, psychological, social, and political interactions that make sex such a central, controversial concern in most Western societies.

A second major theme is the importance of eroticism and sensuality to women's lives, their history, their roles in society. Closely connected to this is her conviction that women need to become freer, more powerful, more self-regarding, more aware of the repression inherent in male-dominated, anti-sensual, institutions.

For example, Maraini has deplored the consequences of Catholic education that teaches negative attitudes about sexuality, and gives no information to women about their bodies. As mothers, she believes, women often perpetuate these values. They teach their children that for women sex is a sin, that motherhood is a woman's only means of social expression, and that a good mother sacrifices all for her children.

'The autonomy women found in religious orders was purchased by subordination to the church,' Maraini has said.[1] 'Women's power, to bring forth life, venerated in ancient times, has been appropriated by the fathers of church and society. Sexual freedom for women is condemned while sexual liberty of men is considered a sign of virility and of independence.'[2]

---

1 Lucia Chiavola Birnbaum, *Liberazione della donna: Feminism in Italy* (Wesleyan University, 1986), p. 196.
2 *Op. cit.,* p. 114.

Maraini claims that women 'often tend to internalize the values invented for them by the Great Fathers of Western thought. Actually, men have always asked women to be fragile and dependent. Often, out of love or generosity, women have taken on both qualities. In this situation, women are sometimes led to disparage other women, considering them parts of a world of submission and loss of self. But those who disparage other women also do not know how to leave that world. Having little regard for themselves, they end by having little regard for others.'

Maraini has fought against this repression and misunderstanding through her writing, in several ways. One way, which forms a third theme in her work, is her prolific use of images and details of everyday life most closely associated with women: the sounds and smells of the home – of food, kitchen, bed, of clothing, of one's own body. Maraini sees these mundane, personal details of life as characteristic of the experiences of women in all classes. She sees their elevation into our literary and political consciousness as important to the recognition and honoring of women's true experiences.

In the same vein, she frequently writes in forms most typical of women's past writings, which have not usually been considered literature, such as letters and private journals.

Most of her novels are written in the first person. *Donna in guerra* is written in the form of a diary kept by Vanina, a young, married schoolteacher who goes with her husband to vacation in the south of Italy. *Lettere a Marina* is a series of letters written by one woman to another. *La lunga vita di Marianna Ucria* is the story of a deaf-mute woman of the 18th Century, daughter of a noble Palermo family, who is constrained either to marry to enhance her family's fortunes or to enter a convent. Marianna writes on a portable tablet in order to communicate, and the novel records her thoughts. Through such works Maraini is helping to bring these vehicles of women's self-expression more fully into literary recognition.

More broadly, Mariani works to change women's place in the world through her use of language, and this is the fourth major theme that I see in her work. In poetry, in novels, and especially in the theatre, language is for her a means to open people's minds and feelings, to help both women and men see and feel new dimensions of our experience.

In her novels, poems, and plays, Maraini is uninhibited in her use of explicit sexual language. People often tell of their surprise, after meeting her. As one said: 'She's so feminine, so sweet, gracious, and gentle. I didn't expect her to be like that from reading her work.' But Maraini uses sexual language for several purposes: as a metaphor to reveal character; as a way to show that sex roles and sexual behavior are the result of socialization; to underscore the relation between sexual attitudes and violence towards women; and to make present and verbal women's desire and capacity for sexual gratification – as described and defined by women.

'Language is a living organism,' she has written, 'and it has a sex. It is not an anonymous tool which can be used by everyone in the same way. Language has its own symbolic system. Within its structure, language holds the ancient vision of the world which formed it ... '

Maraini notes that women have written little, either in plays or in prose, about eroticism. Perhaps, she says, this is because achieving the liberty to write at all was such an audacious victory that women feared obscuring or polluting their work with the suspicion of obscenity.

It may also be because women have, in the main, written about themselves. 'Love's cry, the sweetness of a dreamed awaiting, the deliriums of a mind devastated by self-oppression, religious sublimation' – these have been the fields of women's writing. Eroticism, Maraini says, is about the desired, the other, the mysterious. To write about it, women need a freedom that they never had in the past – to explore their ideas and criticisms of the other, including the erotic, as they have actually experienced it.

In winning such freedoms, will women have to learn, like men, to separate sex from sentiment, pleasure from love? Is that necessary in order for women to choose sex for itself, for themselves, rather than being 'taken over' by it? Maraini has written: 'Frankly, I can't answer ... And I do not feel like giving judgments [nor trying to] establish how women could and should write for the theatre. It is enough for me that they do it and always with more freedom ... I don't think that women are more kind or purer than men. They are contradictory, they know evil and must decide, with free responsibility, whether to choose joy or pain, cheerfulness or melancholy, the giving or the taking.'

How She Works

Dacia Maraini works at her writing every day from 9 a.m. to 2 p.m. That schedule is not unlike that of many other writers. What is unusual is that, on some days, Maraini writes poetry; on other days, she works on a novel, or on a drama, a screenplay, or a critical essay.

The making of a novel, Maraini has said, is like constructing a ten-story building. 'One must have an engineering knowledge. It is a complex project and it takes many years to be completed.' And the poem? 'That is like pitching a tent: One finds a place, opens the tent, sleeps there; then one picks it up and goes away. But writing a play for the theatre is like digging a well: One works vertically, going down deep.'

For Maraini, each idea is born in its form. Ideas for poems emerge as poems, although many of her poems are narratives. 'I am a storyteller,' she says. 'I hear the rhythm of the words in my ear.' She does not use rhyme, but depends on the rhythmic structure of the language, which she works and reworks by hand, writing and re-writing the poem and reading it aloud to herself many times.

The novel, for Maraini, has at its center the 'mystery of time ... '

'Through the use of descriptive language it allows us to stop, look, admire, and contemplate. Its grammar is the imperfect tense: 'Once upon a time there was ... ' Why are we born, why do we live and die? Why does time seem to us our master and at the same time abstract and indifferent? This feeling of the passage of time, at the same time enigmatic and cruel, senseless and seductive, is at the foundation of the writing of every novel. The same narrative form, with its descriptions, its reasons, its pauses, its metamorphoses, its accelerations and decelerations, is a mocking imitation of life, with its own long, rhythmic steps. Every story told is in miniature a theory of the universe. It is an attempt to explain, through the thousand possibilities of description, the pitiless passage of time, which brings us anguish and sadness while at the same time it exalts and charms us.'

The novel, Maraini says, is like the film in structure. It is based on the relationship of space between the narrator and narrative material, which allows distance, irony.

Maraini on Theatre and Language

'The structure of theatre is the present,' Maraini has written, 'a combination of thought and action. Everything is symbolic in theatre; there is no irony, no distance. Action is its mode. In the theatre, language is charged, transformed into metaphor. Even as the lighting used in theatre is visible, because we can see its source, artifice, superimposed on the human, the natural, and the poetic, creates a dramatic language. Dialogue is the essence of theatre and the language of theatre ... Through dialogue, structure becomes characters and ideas ... Dialogue is the flesh and blood of character.'

Maraini believes that theatre should allow the audience to discover the joy and sensuality of language, to 'play with the mother's body.' Words are connected to thought, to inquiry, to the daily transformation of one's native language, and to one's self.

Because of her strong sense of the centrality of language, Maraini believes that Italian theatre must use Italian dialogue, centered in and developed from geographically defined knowledge. 'We have so little respect and regard for the work being done in that newly-born, carefully nurtured, rickety child that is the Italian language,' she says. She insists that written language is not the same as spoken language, and that one cannot write without having a direct and vital relationship to one's own language, the language actually used in one's own country. The language of theatre, while it mimics spoken language, 'utilizes rhythm which heightens one's awareness of the complexity of the reality of which it speaks.'

The language of the theatre is particularly sexist because of the theatre's history: The stage, she reminds us, was the sacred space from which women were excluded. Women's bodies have always been used in theatre, but women have been absent, and also absent has been the expression of their desires. The erotic language of theatre uses women's bodies to evoke men's desires and usually excludes women as thinking subjects.

'The woman has been used as an image without dimension,' Maraini has said.

'In the birthplace of theatre, we saw the male Greek actor-playwright transform himself into Clytemnestra or Medea or Phædra by simply changing masks ... The Greeks considered the stage a sacred place, but the Romans considered the theatre a place of 'ludus' [play, sport] ... It had nothing sacred about it, as it had in Greece. In fact, the Greek plays were enacted by poets and playwrights, while the Roman Atellan farces were enacted by male slaves. This made a great difference in the goals of the theatre in society ... In the late decadent Roman theatre, women were sometimes accepted on stage, but only as apparitions of beauty and sexual desire, not as real, actual performers. According to the principle of 'actor primarium patrium,' the primary [male Roman] actor arrogated all the roles of queen and goddess ... In the Mystery plays of the Middle Ages, the priests disguised themselves as Madonna or saint. Women were admitted only as spectators; that is, as faithful and subdued repentants ... It was only during the Renaissance that the female body took its place on the stage. This evoked the malediction of the Church,

which accused actresses of bestiality, pro-
miscuity, relationship with the Devil, prostitution, and heresy, and refused them burial
in consecrated ground.'

We have no texts, Maraini notes, from this
teatro allo improviso, or *teatro dell'arte,* as it was
later called.

'But the principle of women's freedom at
the time was conceived only as the freedom
to choose a husband, who remained the
being to whom the woman owed absolute
and legal obedience. This principle was
introduced into theatre as an idea which
achieved great popularity and success. In
the centuries following, in music and theatre
(from Pergolesi to Beaumarchais, from
Rossini to Molière) many others have dealt
with this theme. Above all, it was Goldoni
who in his plays portrayed women as resolute
in demanding their interests – to have
husbands not chosen by their fathers, to
inherit and manage their own money, not
to be forced into nunneries against their
wills, to be able to separate from violent
husbands ... Goldoni was one of the few male
playwrights to show the woman's world with
realism and sympathy. Only Ibsen, among
modern playwrights, did much the same.'

La Maddalena

In 1973, Maraini decided to start her own theatre collective, and women's theatre was born that year in Rome, under the name La Maddalena. In those years, the Italian theatre was totally in the hands of men. Women were only accepted as actresses, assistants, or costumers. There was no place where women could confront and discuss their ideas. The goal of the Maddalena group was to create a space where women could express themselves personally as directors, playwrights, and musicians.

In the center of Rome, nestled between the Pantheon and the House of Parliament, on a cobblestone street called 'The Street of the Little Star,' Maraini and her colleagues formed a women's theatre group collective. Thirty women, working together, rented the basement of an old typographer's workshop, painted the walls, and built a stage.

The beginning, Maraini recalls, was difficult, particularly the technology of theatre. There were no women who were capable of dealing with stage lighting or sound systems. So La Maddalena formed a school for technicians and, within a few months, had trained women to handle the technical aspects of theatre.

The Maddalena cooperators set up new procedures for their work, insisting that each text considered for production was to be read publicly and discussed in front of the writer, until all agreed on the text that was to be performed.

For a number of years, the group staged four or five plays each season. The productions were inexpensively mounted, emphasing dramatic structure over scenography. When the government began to raise taxes, and made heavy cuts in its subsidies to small theatres, La Maddalena struggled to survive by reducing its productions, first from five to three and then from three to one per year. At last, unable to produce at all, the group turned to running seminars on acting, directing, and playwrighting, calling on some of Italy's best theatre actresses and women directors.

For sixteen years, from 1973 until 1989, La Maddalena served as a theatre group and a theatre space that was also a forum for political ideas and action. Women have used it to meet and discuss and organize other meetings, both national and international, on subjects of importance to women: violence, family, love, abortion, prostitution. The group was an important part of the efforts that have won a number of battles for civil rights in Italy in recent years. For example, in the intensely Catholic nation of Italy, women in 1978 gained the legal right to an abortion on demand.

La Maddalena also organized theatre festivals,

with other groups composed only of women. Participating groups have included 'Spider-woman' from New York, the London Women's Theatre Group, and 'Les montreuses d'images' from Berne, as well as women's groups from all over Italy, including 'Teatro di l'elfo' from Milan, 'Gruppo commedia' from Florence, 'Il collectivo 15 donne' from Turin, and the 'Gruppo ragazze da marito' (Girls To Be Married) from Verona.

La Maddalena's actresses performed 'street theatre' in Rome's markets and piazzas, and travelled throughout Italy with backpacks, performing in smaller cities and towns. Looking back, Maraini has said 'We had enthusiasm and certainties which are now lost.'

Manya Kochansky describes Maraini as 'the steady, intelligent, unrelenting, smiling, non-violent figure' who presided over the group. Kochansky, an author-actress, created a perform-ance piece based on her life, which she presented through the Maddalena group. 'La Maddalena not only gave me a stage,' she has written. 'It gave me another gift even more precious: The Group.'

Strong friendships developed quickly within the Maddalena group, energized by a shared love of theatre. Maraini speaks now of the group's maternal character, and the participants' 'obsessive request for maternal care ... The group was the mother and everyone wanted to be loved blindly by her. But they, for their own parts, didn't want to love blindly at all. Only mothers love unconditionally, and each one asked to be treated as a daughter but did not wish to be a mother – that is, to love blindly, without arguing, without judging, without differentiating.'

Maraini's Vision of the Future

A similar sense of ongoing struggle and complexity pervades Maraini's writing. Maraini often depicts women struggling to shake off the shackles of their internalized, male attitudes and values as sexual beings. The women protagonists of her works must struggle against their own senses of dependency, shame, guilt, isolation, and fear of being unloved, in order to avoid betraying their own natures.

Thus Vanina, the elementary school teacher in *Woman At War,* finds that her war against a male-oriented society requires her not only to liberate herself from an oppressive marriage but also to teach others, male and female, a way of cooperating to change the social structure of that society. Maraini's Mary Stuart, Queen of Scots, struggles to balance her feminine instincts to love and bear children with the demand to hold a position of power and authority in a male world, which makes a slave even of a queen. Manila, the prostitute in *Dialogue between a*

Prostitute and her Client, confuses herself and her client into asking 'Who's the customer here?' Because she can understand and identify with him, she endangers their business contract, which is designed only to provide pleasure to the client, and only through the sexual act.

Women in Maraini's work are finding their strength by getting back in touch with their bodies. This connection harkens back to deep, non-verbal places, reminding women that they are sentient beings, for whom the relationship to the body is a profound one. In *Woman At War,* Vanina awakens to the flow of her menstrual blood while lying in the sun – a symbolic stirring that launches her into a fuller awareness of her deepest self. In *Mary Stuart,* Mary embraces herself, her hands caress her own body, while Elizabeth takes pleasure from looking at the naked body of a young boy, saying that 'since the queen has no body she derives her satisfaction from other people's.' Manila, in *Dialogue,* feels her breasts full of milk, which pours down her client's throat, symbolically becoming Manila herself. She in turn becomes him, thirsting for his mother's milk, and she is also the milk. The mother and the son and his seed and her milk – all blend into the bodily juices of interconnection, the commingling of male and female, of giving and receiving. The juices of the human body become a river that courses between people, binding them and melding them together.

All of the women in Maraini's works are, sexually and personally, potentially powerful people. The reader or audience member is able to feel and participate in their attempts to gain control of, make sense of, their lives and loves.

Success is not theirs; only the beginning, the possibility of success. For example, Manila's client takes pleasure from her psycho-sexual immersion in his wishes and needs, and uses her affection for him to cheat her. Her sister-prostitutes attack him as he leaves with the glib throw-away line: 'Getting rid of prostitution is part of the new morality. 'Manila is left to comfort her crying baby with a sad closing lullaby:

'Sleep tight, don't worry about your future.
I'll sew your lips together with string
So you won't be tempted to kiss anyone.
I'll sew up your cunt with silken thread
So you won't be tempted to fuck anyone.'

Yet Maraini's women find ways to hope. Mary Stuart is also cheated, and later beheaded. Before she goes to her death, she gives a medallion carrying the portrait of her mother to her loyal companion and lady-in-waiting, Kennedy, with the words '[R]emember that ties between women are the strongest and most lasting.' She vows to 'journey in the snow-white silence of the eternal dream.'

Clytemnestra, in the play *The Dreams of Clytemnestra,* dies 'in the name of truth and family order,' as Moira – Fury, prostitute, apparition – chants:

'Oh, how they have suffered
How they have suffered
Unhappy daughters of the night,
Daughters all wounded.'

But Clytemnestra, too, vows that 'Somewhere, among dead dreams, I will keep on living, to keep on dreaming.'

Hope, yes, but only for the future. The letter-writer in the novel *Lettere a Marina* comes to a new understanding of herself in the process of writing to another woman. In writing fully about her relationship to another person, she discovers more fully her own identity.

In Maraini's 1990 novel, *The Silent Duchess,* the 18th Century heroine, made deaf and mute by sexual violation, can still express herself through writing. She also is surrounded by other women – daughters, grandmothers, servant women, midwives – who find their own ways to resist the violent and oppressive patriarchy of their time.[1]

---

1 Lucia Chiavola Birnbaum, *Black madonnas. Feminism, Religion, and Politics in Italy.* Boston: Northeastern University Press, 1993.

From her writing and from her life, Maraini's vision seems to be that women can change their lives, but they must first claim the right of self-expression and then forge bonds of mutual help and support with other women.

> ' ... a destiny of red silk
> unites women of all classes
> we are covered by ancient rustling leaves
> madonnas with amputated fingers
> students with star teeth
> housewives with flaking hands
> wealthy ladies with raffia purses
> girls who masturbate with peach fingers
> old bigot women with tough eyes ...
> the body of a woman who is thinking
> shakes the scaled back of history.' [2]

2 From 'A Body of Woman', in Dacia Maraini, *Devour Me Too,* translated by Genni Donati Gunn (Montreal: Guernica Editions), 1978, with emendations by Dacia Maraini.

Mary Stuart

Freely adapted from
Mary Stuart by Friedrich Von Schiller
Translated by Christopher Pearcy
with Nicolette Kay

Preface

Mary Stuart covers a nineteen-year period during which the Queen of Scots was a prisoner of Elizabeth, Queen of England. Two actresses are on stage; each plays both a queen and a lady companion to the other queen. Hence Elizabeth is sometimes transformed into Kennedy, Mary's companion, and Mary is also Nanny, Elizabeth's lady in waiting. The companions exist only by the grace of their queens. They behave as traditional dependent females: obedient, concerned, caring. The queens and their servants are equally forced to deny their bodies, and all have been subjected to physical and psychological isolation – despite their vastly differing social classes. Although the two queens never meet in the play, we see how they control each other's lives. Elizabeth keeps Mary in physical confinement, but she must attempt desperately to justify Mary's imprisonment. At the same time, Mary sends Elizabeth letters of devotion, requesting a meeting. It is as if they share an irresistible attraction for each other.

Mary, whom we meet in prison, is a shadow of the dynamic queen she has been. Compassionate, intuitive, and emotional, she had lived trying to be a queen and at the same time a feminine person. As she relives her past, we learn what has led to her deterioration. Elizabeth, by contrast, appears as a powerful woman. But in order to keep her dominance in her kingdom, she hides her needs, desires, and vulnerability behind a mask that is imposed on her by politics. The same society that forces this mask on her judges her harshly for being unmarried and childless. Each of the two women recognizes in the other that part of herself that has been brutally suppressed.

In a patriarchal society, Maraini's play suggests, the social roles allotted to women consist of producing new members of society, caring for them, and educating them in traditional values. Many women are content to fulfill these traditional roles inside the home; others are not. Many are unhappy, not because they look down on the traditional roles, but because they have not been allowed a choice whether to play them.

In Maraini's view, if a woman is successful in the 'outside' world, people wonder about her lack of femininity, her egotism, and her assumed failure to take care of others (a husband and children). A woman who tries to balance the inside and outside worlds runs the risk of being crushed between the demands of the two.

The play ends with the beheading of Mary, as described by Kennedy. Mary thinks of her death as a release. Elizabeth, having signed the death warrant, not only kills her cousin, but also kills her feelings about what it means to be a woman.

This play has had many successful productions throughout the world. Besides Italy, it has been performed in Australia, Austria, Belgium, France, Holland, Japan, Spain, and Uruguay. A first version was produced in English in England in 1984, translated by Christopher Pearcy and Nicolette Kay, with Olivia Brown as Elizabeth and Niki Kay as Mary. It was performed as a one-woman adaptation in Portuguese at La Mama E.T.C. in New York by Brazilian actress Denise Staklos. It was performed for the first time in English in the United States at California State University, Hayward in 1990, with Jennifer Hurd as Elizabeth and Elicia Young as Mary, directed by Rhoda Helfman Kaufman.

Characters

Mary Stuart
Queen of Scotland

Elizabeth
Queen of England

Kennedy
Lady-in-waiting to Mary Stuart

Nanny
Lady-in-waiting to Elizabeth

(The four parts can be played by just two actresses. When one plays the Queen the other plays her interlocutor and vice-versa.)

ACT I

MARY

Bring me my mirror.

KENNEDY

Paulet took it away. He said a prisoner shouldn't enjoy her own image.

MARY

Come in front of me, Kennedy.

Kennedy kneels in front of Mary.

MARY

How is my hair?

KENNEDY

Brown, shiny, thick.

MARY

I didn't ask you to flatter me. How is it?

KENNEDY

Thin.

MARY

And?

KENNEDY

Dull.

MARY

And?

KENNEDY

Turning grey.

MARY

How are my eyes?

KENNEDY

Large, gentle, luminous.

MARY

Liar!

She strikes her.

KENNEDY

Dark.

MARY

And?

KENNEDY

Tired, angry, red.

MARY

They're dead.

KENNEDY

They're beautiful, I promise you ... you've always looked at me through those eyes and I've learnt to know everything that goes on behind them ...

MARY

You're wrong, Kennedy, whatever you say, you're wrong. If you tell the truth you're wrong because you treat me like a stranger. If you lie you're wrong because you treat me like a fool.

KENNEDY

Would you like a lime tisane?

MARY

Your tisanes make me vomit.

KENNEDY

Would your like your prayer-book?

MARY

And do you know what's in your eyes? Fear, submission, apprehension, sagacity, goodness, a suffocating irritating goodness. Don't look at me anymore. Go to the kitchen! No, go to Paulet instead and ask him if there's been a letter from my beloved cousin Elizabeth.

KENNEDY

Your beloved cousin detests you. And as soon as she can she'll have you executed.

MARY

She wears a medallion round her neck with my portrait on it.

KENNEDY

She deceives you.

MARY

On her finger she wears the heart-shaped diamond I sent her when I arrived in Scotland.

KENNEDY

She only wants your death.

MARY

How do you know what goes on in a queen's heart! Go and make me a lime tisane, go ... go, idiot, go!

Kennedy goes out.

MARY

How swollen you are mother.

She speaks to an imaginary phantom.

Ambassador Beaton had told me about it but I never imagined until now ... The Queen your mother no longer wears the pearls you gave her round her neck because she feels she's suffocating ... your lips are swollen and your belly's taut ...

it is the longing for your two children who were taken from you ... a bilious, watery, bleak yearning for motherhood ... But you were always proud, perversely, insolently proud ... like the time they brought me back to you after two months' absence and you leapt forward to embrace me, trembling with emotion, but a quick glance at the courtiers gave you to understand that this was not the way for a queen to behave and you withdrew like a hedgehog. You lifted your pale face above me, held out your hand and said softly : How is my lady daughter?

Imitating her mother.

You are not a child Mary, you are a crown ... your body is not for playing games, you are a statue. When you speak, you do not speak for yourself but for your country ... Nothing must happen to you but that you wish it ... Nothing must disturb your sensibility that is not sanctioned by Parliament!

* * *

ELIZABETH

Bring me my mirror, Nanny.

NANNY

It was broken a moment ago.

ELIZABETH

And did you throw salt on it?

NANNY

I sent for another straight away.

ELIZABETH

Two strokes of the whip for whoever broke it. Who dropped it?

NANNY

You, Your Majesty.

ELIZABETH

Well then, two strokes of the whip for me. Who is prepared to beat the Queen and then be hung for lèse-majesté?

NANNY

Would Your Majesty like me to borrow a mirror from one of your courtiers?

ELIZABETH

I shall reflect myself in those icy eyes of yours, Nanny. How's my hair?

NANNY

Rich, curly, golden.

ELIZABETH

Well done, you've learned to lie gracefully ...
And my lips?

NANNY

Soft, full, gentle.

ELIZABETH

You have forgotten sensual.

NANNY

As you please ... but to me, your lips seem to be
more volatile than sensual.

ELIZABETH

So, I wouldn't make a good lover. Is that what
you think?

NANNY

As you've upset the Court, by refusing all possible
husbands, it can only mean you're afraid of the
marriage bed.

ELIZABETH

You know every man believes himself to be a
king because he has a natural sceptre ... now
think of a man with a sceptre of flesh and one
of gold and rubies ... I don't want to be like
that idiot, my cousin Mary. She fell in love with
a beanpole ... and he with his peacock's tail ...
He had so many whims, that in the end they
killed him.

NANNY

They say it was she who killed him.

ELIZABETH

Even if she had, she had every reason ... Didn't he try to kill her with his child inside her? ... How are my eyes?

NANNY

Brilliant, bold.

ELIZABETH

Can't you think of anything else?

NANNY

It's a mortal sin to kill your husband.

ELIZABETH

Not for a queen. Didn't my father kill his wife? ... and nobody had anything to say against that ... Everybody's prepared to find the right excuse ... Mary lacks imagination ... Your eyes, Your Majesty, are two vases full of turquoise honey.

She curtsies.

That's what you ought to say, fool! ... As you lean forward, the honey falls upon my hands staining them blue ...

NANNY

Your eyes are ... But why do you want me to tell lies, when you know that's what they are?

ELIZABETH

Lies are the seal of your subjection ... the more you tell me lies the more you are subject to me ... the Court must lie to show it's awe of the Royal House ... Heaven help them if they speak the truth.

NANNY

There are the drums! May I go to the window to watch the execution?

ELIZABETH

You're too honest, Nanny, you'll end up at the stake!

NANNY

They're undressing him ... what a handsome lad ... he can only be about twenty ... he's got a head tattooed on his right arm ... the head of a medusa ...

ELIZABETH

I'm sick of these exhibitions ...

NANNY

Now the executioner is blindfolding him ...

45

Drums.

Now four of them are holding him against the block ... Now the executioner is thrusting the knife into his chest ... ah! a single stroke with a sure hand ... the boy's shuddering ... the four men are spattered with blood ... now the executioner has ripped out his heart and is holding it up high ... the people are applauding ... how delicate this executioner is ... he's taking the innards out as if they were pieces of silver for the Queen's table ... now he's looking up at your window ...

ELIZABETH

What was he accused of?

NANNY

Sodomy ...

ELIZABETH

It's barbaric ...

NANNY

A lovely execution ... The crowd's delirious. They're chanting your name ... a lovely execution ... the boy's still moving his feet ... They're waiting for you.

ELIZABETH

All excess horrifies me ...

NANNY

But it's the law that prescribes it ...

ELIZABETH

Laws are made to be changed, Nanny. I can change them. I will change them.

* * *

MARY

I'm tired ... I've just travelled forty miles on horse back ... with child, you understand, with child ... and what if I abort? If I abort the future king of Scotland? ... Where's his father? Where's that degenerate Henry, where is he? Out hunting, out hunting ... with Countess Veronica ... or with the blacksmith's daughter, Catherine? When he was confined to his bed, with syphilis, I never left his side! Now I'm about to give birth and he's not here! Call him, tell him wherever he may be, to leave everything and come to his wife the Queen, who is about to give him a child ... I want him to be here to recognize it and to give it the customary blessing.

KENNEDY

You're talking to yourself!

MARY

I'm keeping myself company.

KENNEDY

A letter.

MARY

From Elizabeth?

KENNEDY

From Mortimer. But be careful, if they find it here, we are lost you and I ...

MARY

Reading.

'Adored Mary, I am on my way from France where I have seen your dearest friends. They all want you to be free. They are suffering for your imprisonment which offends the whole Catholic world. Although I have never seen you, I have been in love with you ever since your portrait came into my hands at the house of Bishop Ross in Rheims. Have faith in me and in the Pope. We will set you free. Keep yourself prepared ...' I will kiss this Mortimer on the mouth. Is he handsome?

KENNEDY

Tall, fair ... but not washed out like your husband Darnley ... his colour is fiery and splendid ...

MARY

Tell him to be careful. We are surrounded here by hundreds of guards ... Paulet keeps watch night and day ...

KENNEDY

Mortimer wants a pledge from you ... A response.

MARY

Give him this ring ... Tell him to go to the Earl of Leicester, the handsome Lord Robert ... He will find a friend in him ... He must tell him that I sent him ... My freedom can only come from him, or the queen ... go, run ...

ELIZABETH

You, dear John ... no ... you, dear Hawkins ... no ... you, Hawkins are proposing that I finance an expedition of piracy ... no ... that's not right ... dearest Hawkins, I have read your letter ... you are right ... the Americas are the new world, we can benefit greatly from the Americas ... and God calls upon us to carry civilization and morality into these barbaric countries ... as far as the blacks you are taking from Africa to sell in the markets of new world ... no, no, here we need to be diplomatic and regal ... as for the wild beasts which you have had the kindness to dissuade from their loathsome habits and hand over to the Anglican church, are concerned ...

well I can do as I please ... I'll pay for five ships so that you can leave quickly and return as soon as possible laden with glory and riches ... so... bah!

NANNY

Coming in.

Have you thought about your marriage, Your Majesty?

ELIZABETH

What's that got to do with anything?

NANNY

A delegation of merchants have come this morning, to bring you a magnificent wedding present ...

ELIZABETH

Bloody hell, what do these shit-arses want from me?

NANNY

Your Majesty, they can hear you ...

ELIZABETH

Let them hear me ... seeing that they treat me like a washerwoman ... I'll answer like a wash-erwoman ... What's the difference between me and a peasant woman? She is asked to take a husband and bear a son ... I am asked to take a husband and bear a son ...

NANNY

If you were to die without an heir, the throne would fall to Mary, a Catholic. The Protestant people fear for their security ... you know very well what your step-sister Mary Tudor did when she came to the throne after Edward ...

ELIZABETH

I know ... the bonfires, all London in flames ... every night hundreds of Protestants captured, slaughtered, disemboweled alive. Once, from my window, I saw a young boy of sixteen in the palace courtyard being maimed with red-hot irons ... people were roaring ... some whispered prayers, others bought fritters, drank wine ... it was like holiday ... she was standing there wearing a gown of black brocade fastened up to the neck, eyes of stone, her hands clutching the window-sill like talons ... she looked as if she was watching her own body being ripped to pieces ...

NANNY

Fortunately you're so different ...

ELIZABETH

Perhaps she was more like my father the execu-tioner than I am ...

NANNY

Nevertheless your father made the greatest revolution in English history, he freed the country from the yoke of Catholicism.

ELIZABETH

Without realizing it, through egotism, through idiocy. When he saw what he'd done he became scared. He only wanted to change his wife.

NANNY

Now everybody's grateful for his political astuteness ...

ELIZABETH

He only wanted to fuck whoever he pleased ... but with full rights ... so he rejected Catherine of Aragon, the most beautiful boiled fish, for the volcanic Anne Boleyn, my mother; but then even Anne began to irritate him and he had her executed in order to marry the extremely dull, extremely devout, Jane Seymour who thought quite rightly to die a natural death before she too began to irritate him ...

NANNY

It's not good to hate your own father.

ELIZABETH

I don't hate him. I judge him : a flea-brained vandal.

NANNY

No one says your marriage would be like your mother's ...

ELIZABETH

I remember when she used to come into my bedroom before I went to sleep ... I waited for her ... I heard her shoes on the wooden floor ... her perfume of violets mixed with sweat ... the lovely Anne Boleyn never walked ... she ran with her neck stretched out before her, that slender neck, which was severed by that axe ... zac! ... when she leant over me she breathed quickly, her cheeks damp with sweat ... zac! her head fell into the box ... you know I've always been afraid of opening boxes ... I'm convinced that I'll find my mother's head inside.

NANNY

The people are asking you to take a husband.

ELIZABETH

You will tell the French Ambassador that he may bring the marriage proposals from his Lord, King Charles III. I will listen to him patiently. I will offer him sherberts, beer from my cellars ... I will make him the gift of a ring ... many rings make a chain ... but I'll give him only one and for a year we'll dally ... then I'll tell him no.

NANNY

If foreign princes scare you, why don't you marry Lord Dudley, your cupbearer, your favourite?

ELIZABETH

Robert is made of the same stuff as Darnley. A beautiful body with a pathetic brain. He can only bear cups.

NANNY

You have made him the Earl of Leicester ... giving him land and castles.

ELIZABETH

He'll have more land and more castles but he won't have the title of King.

NANNY

There's also the Spanish Ambassador who is asking to be received to make a proposal of marriage on behalf of his Lord, Don Carlos.

ELIZABETH

They say he's epileptic, ugly as sin, a hunchback and black ... but that doesn't matter ... do you want me to turn England into a coffer for Philip II like that vulture Mary Tudor did? She married Philip and then he made her give him thousands of pounds to finance his wars against France ... just to lose them like the dimwit he is ...

NANNY

If you don't marry, Mary Stuart's right to the throne will become stronger. The aristocracy will make you condemn her to death.

ELIZABETH

I will never sign the death warrant of a sister who puts so much trust in me.

NANNY

Well, marry!

ELIZABETH

Go, Nanny, don't irritate me ...

* * *

MARY

Huntley, you lump of lard! Come down! He didn't want to open the gates to his queen. James, stop looking like a Buddha because you haven't had your lands yet ... they say I'm making a mistake ... who says so? I say so, I tell you that you're clearing the North of all your possible allies ... Huntley is a Catholic, he has immense power ... destroy him and you destroy your

potential allies on protestant ground ... and I
tell you, Miss Know-it-all, you're making a
mistake ... Huntley has insulted his queen ... he
has stolen the royal furnishings from the chapel
at Aberdeen, he has killed, robbed and plotted ...
a subject like that can never be useful ... Now
I'm here with three thousand men, his castle is
be sieged, but he won't come out ... he's assem-
bling his forces ... you puffed-up balloon
Huntley, you lard-face, come and fight if you're
brave enough! ... Lord, how bold the queen is
on her horse! At the head of her men, hair in
the wind, without armour ... inciting them,
spurring them on ... the others were tired after
endless hours at the gallop in the rain ... not she
... she with her fragile shoulders draped in red
velvet, bounded forward dragging her army in
her wake ... Huntley wanted to kidnap her and
marry her. Kidnap and marry. The barrel of
lard. It was prophesied that before nightfall, the
very noble Lord Huntley would lie in the Tollbooth at Aberdeen, without a wound on his
body. Sleeping? Resting? How beautiful the
Queen was, her face flushed by the gallop as she
led her soldiers! The brave Lord James, the
Queen's brother, killed two of Huntley's sons
and captured a third together with his father.
He brought them before Queen Mary. You,
Queen, have betrayed your religion ... may you
be cursed! And you, piece of shit, you have

betrayed yourself. At that precise moment Huntley fell from his horse dead as a doornail. The witches had said that he would die without wounds, that he would die intact and lie peacefully within the Tollbooth ...

* * *

ELIZABETH

Right Hawkins! ... no, stronger ; you, Lieutenant of the London Sewers ... hm ... perhaps not ... cold. Admiral John Hawkins, you are reduced to the rank of able seaman ... Bloody Hawkins, how dare you attack my illustrious brother-in-law Philip II's ships and take the treasure he'd stolen from the Americas? ... you think I don't know how you get hold of Blacks, how you hunt them, how you load them and the way you carry them in the holds of your foul ships? I know your greed...

— But, Your Majesty, you know how much the treasury benefits from the trade in Blacks ...
— Call it the trade of human flesh ... which you exchange for gold, silver and precious stones.
— The crown is greatly enriched by this gold, Your Majesty.
— Right, but you must not be caught. If you are caught you are an imbecile and an outlaw. And as such you will lose the favour of the Crown. You are under arrest, John Hawkins!

Enter Nanny.

ELIZABETH

Nanny, yesterday in the stables, I saw a youth with sparkling eyes. Bring him here.

NANNY

The French Ambassador's here with gifts ...

ELIZABETH

Later, Nanny, later. Go and find that youth.

Nanny goes.

ELIZABETH

I have three thousand clothes but nothing suits me ... boots of pigskin, dogskin ... brocade, damask, velvet ... there are parts of myself I never see ... they say one is born naked ... when I have a bath, I have four strong women around me who rub me with salt, scents and soap ... I'm getting old and I don't know what's happening to my body ...

As if the door has opened.

Ah, here's the sparrow ... come in, come in, don't be frightened ... how handsome you are! What's your name? Has the cat got your tongue? It doesn't matter, keep silent ... your lovely arms say more about you than your name could ... now undress ... yes, undress I command you. I only want to look at you ... As the Queen has no body, she satisfies herself with other peoples' ... you are white and slim and well-built ... now kneel here and kiss my feet ... And ... now dress yourself and go back to the stables. Nanny, give him two crowns ... and show the French Ambassador in ...

* * *

MARY

My voice leaves my mouth to enter my ear ... my hand moves away from my shoulder to caress ... my cheek ... my right foot brushes my left foot ...

Enter Kennedy.

MARY

Any news, Kennedy? A letter from Elizabeth?

KENNEDY

No letters. Elizabeth will never see you. If she saw you she would never be able to sentence you to death.

MARY

Kennedy, in this prison, I'm condemned to feed on myself ... I remember hearing about a boy buried alive in an earthquake who saved himself by drinking his own urine. But how long can one survive consuming one's own secretions?

KENNEDY

I am here, my Queen, you can talk to me.

MARY

You are my reflection ... can't you hear that you speak with my voice, you think with my head ... you are the soft predictable impression that my body leaves on things.

KENNEDY

I followed you from Scotland, I left my husband and children for you ...

MARY

Exactly ... without me you would not exist ... didn't you tell me that one of your teeth is rotting, the right molar?

KENNEDY

What's that got to do with anything?

MARY

Two months after mine had started to rot, the same molar ... do you remember what the surgeon said?

KENNEDY

I don't remember ... I didn't like his face, he looked like a hypocrite ...

MARY

He looked like a well-paid surgeon ... those wrinkles are from the pleasure other people's pain has brought him ... there is a deep melancholy pleasure in the observation of other people's pain ...

KENNEDY

Would you like me to make you a mint tisane?

MARY

'The root of this tooth is embedded in the hard terrain of your heart ... if it rots it means that something in that terrain is putrefying'... That's what the surgeon said, and you pretend not to remember ...

KENNEDY

You're too tired ... you are tormenting yourself.

MARY

Keeping my own company so much, I've learned to use fewer euphemisms ...

KENNEDY

Perhaps your heart is rotting and you are going bad ...

MARY

If I go bad, the same will happen to you ... we are joined by a spider's web, impalpable but solid and viscous ... a thread made of corruption, love, seduction, jealousy, tenderness ...

KENNEDY

Mortimer swears he'll free you.

MARY

And then he'll want some recompense I imagine ... he will want me to marry him ... what's he like?

KENNEDY

He's tall, robust, eyes like stars, a soft full mouth.

MARY

It's too many years since I last embraced a man ... the continual embracing of myself has emptied me ... However, there is an excitement in simultaneously being the one who embraces and the embraced ... the mirror of perfect symmetry ... the repetition of oneself to infinity ... I will never abandon myself and because of this perhaps I will lose myself, Kennedy ... God wishes one to abandon oneself ...

KENNEDY

It is a blessing to hear you, Your Majesty.

MARY

You see? You can't do anything other than love me ... your love is abject, servile, unnerving ...

KENNEDY

Why are you so cruel to me?

MARY

Because you are part of me, the most defenseless, the most stupid, and to be cruel to this part makes me happy ...

KENNEDY

Well at least you must recognize that you love me too ...

MARY

I don't love you. Kennedy, I possess you. For you, I have that slightly lascivious tenderness that one feels for the more vulnerable parts of one's body.

KENNEDY

Your wicked fantasies have made me forget more important things.

MARY

Elizabeth has asked about me?

KENNEDY

It's about Mortimer ... He's been to see Leicester and ...

MARY

Have you noticed, Kennedy, that when I eat I don't make a noise?

KENNEDY

It's as if you don't want to leave this prison ...

MARY

I drink wine like a ghost ... I eat without making a noise with my throat or tongue ...

KENNEDY

To come to the point. Mortimer went to Leicester with your ring and ...

MARY

You are turning into a ghost too ... when we play piquet in the evening ... how do you think we look, to those who watch us from a distance, behind these dim windows lit by the flickering light of a candle?

KENNEDY

You're delirious ... Mortimer is offering you his hand when you're about to drown and you wander away ...

MARY

Queen Mary of Scotland on horseback followed by her three Maries ... look Kennedy.

She faces the window.

Look at them, how proud and splendid they are! They are going to Parliament ... Mary in front with her black velvet cloak, her plumed hat on her head ... the others behind with golden gloves, buckskin shoes ...

KENNEDY

Mortimer wants to force the prison gates with some Catholic youths ... Leicester does not agree ... he's playing safe ... he wants Elizabeth to meet you, to come to a compromise and give you a passport for France ...

MARY

Mortimer is right, but Leicester is more attractive ... I would be able to meet Elizabeth ...

KENNEDY

I would not trust a man who's a traitor.

MARY

Quick Kennedy, take off my slippers. They pin my feet to the floor ... put on my boots ... I want to go and meet Elizabeth like a queen ...

KENNEDY

It's not something that will happen today or tomorrow ...

MARY

It doesn't matter ... run ... I can feel the blood returning to my veins, run, go and bring me my red brocade skirt ...

* * *

ELIZABETH

You wanted to see me, Robert ... what is it? What ugly wrinkles my mouth makes when I speak ... What does the handsome Lord Dudley want of his queen? ... It's not just because your wife was found dead in bed without any wounds that I haven't married you, Robert ... why don't you ask yourself what the other reasons could be, if you still have any questions left to ask yourself ... I doubt it ... you're too used to just giving answers now ...

Recreating him.

I am dazzled by the sight of you, my dear Elizabeth ... (I bow ... I smile ... shouldn't I smile?) – you are like the joyous dawn of a June day ... – to what do I owe this mawkishness, my Lord? ... you are rich, extremely rich, you also have had the title to which you aspired for so long ... do you too want a ship to trade in Negroes? – Noo ... he is too handsome, dreamy, happy, elegant, too much the lover of comfortable houses and feather beds to cast himself upon the ocean ... Well, my Lord?

I am comparing you in my mind with the Stuart woman ... I will not hide from you that I would like to see you, just once, beside her. Then you would have the ultimate triumph. I would like her to suffer the humiliation of seeing you with her own eyes, and jealousy, believe me, has acute vision ... and you on the other hand standing above her in nobility and stature, you are her superior in deportment, grace and every other quality.

— I look into those muddy eyes that I once loved ... It's probable that I'd let myself try again ... he has the profile of an Apollo, ingratiating, icy ... She is younger than me, Robert ...
— Younger? she doesn't look it ... her sorrows have aged her more than time ... His oily tongue slides about so smoothly under his palate. When she sees you in all your beauty, so full of dignity, illuminated, and almost transfigured, by the aureole of your purity and your virtues, she who has ruined hers and dragged it in the mire ... she wanted to kill you and instead you will kill her ... besides, the art of politics requires that you

see her, that you gain public opinion with an act of generosity. Afterwards, you will be able to free yourself of this hateful enemy as you see fit ...

— How can I deny him anything. Robert with the pretty monkey face ... I shan't say no ... but neither shall I say yes ...

NANNY

You make fun of men ... you're cruel.

ELIZABETH

How dare you speak to me like that!

NANNY

It's the truth.

ELIZABETH

I decide what's the truth.

NANNY

Forgive me.

ELIZABETH

Remember you exist because I wish it.

NANNY

When I was in Sussex I didn't depend on you, I didn't even know what you were like. I did my embroidery in my father's house, I was quite content.

ELIZABETH

You were dependent on your father ... that fatuous, scheming merchant who collects taxes for the Queen ... I know that man too well, Nanny ... he brought you here to placate me ... he sold you to me in exchange for greater freedom from royal control ...

NANNY

Don't say that about my father, he's an honest man and faithful to Your Majesty.

ELIZABETH

I understand men better than you, Nanny. We're both virgins. But you see the world through the eyes of a lady of good family brought up on embroidery, lute and religion ... whilst I ... do you know the story of the sacred grove of Nemos which was guarded by an old priest. He enjoyed all the privileges of a king, but he would only have this power until someone killed him ... So the poor man slept with one eye open. Each night he hid himself in the hollow of a different tree, holding his breath, fear bursting his breast ... on the lookout for the one who was destined to seize and kill him ...

NANNY

I could have stayed at home ...

ELIZABETH

You would have married a man you didn't like to further your father's ambition.

NANNY

I would have had my children.

ELIZABETH

You would have had two masters, your father and your husband ... instead you have only one, me. And I make no claims on your body.

NANNY

My own house ...

ELIZABETH

You're in love with that clown, Major Dexter. I give him to you, Nanny. I will make you a fine dowry. Marry him. If that's what you want, go ahead!

NANNY

I don't care about the Major, even if he would be a good husband ... you know who I'm in love with.

ELIZABETH

I don't know and I don't want to know.

NANNY

You do know.

ELIZABETH

Robert Dudley, my favourite ... But you know
you're risking your head? How dare you be in
love with the Queen's sweetheart ... However if
you're really set on it, do as you please ... you'll
regret it.

NANNY

I want nothing from him. Only to give him my
life.

ELIZABETH

You're a thousand times more intelligent than
he is ... why should you give him your life?

NANNY

I love him.

ELIZABETH

And have you ever asked yourself why you love
my favourite?

NANNY

I told you I want nothing from him.

ELIZABETH

You don't love him, but me ... You love this
game of royal seduction ... this life of expensive
perfumes, watered silk, whale-bone, gold and
emeralds ...

NANNY

You've never loved anybody and can't possibly know ...

ELIZABETH

Love is the consent you give for your own sub-jection ... the enthusiasm which makes you consent to have your blood sucked ... remember the priest of Nemos ... however, Nanny, if it matters so much to you, take him ... he's yours ... his perfume no longer attracts me ... my heart doesn't flutter anymore when I see him ...

* * *

MARY

Riccio, you must stop letting me win ... I'm not stupid ... the Queen of hearts, paff, and you give me the ace of spades ... the ten of clubs and, paff, you give me the two ... I don't like to win like this ... play me something on the lute ... play and sing ... yes, I'll sing as well ...

Song

When the evening is beautiful and dying,
My gentle queen bewitched,
My moth-eyed queen,
There's a black moon within me which dances
When the evening is dark and long,

My fleet-foot queen,
My sparkling eyed queen
You are like the grape and the olive.

KENNEDY

What a lovely voice you have!

MARY

Crow's voice.

KENNEDY

Angel's voice.

MARY

Kennedy, the more you flatter me the more I hate you.

KENNEDY

The more you hate me the more I love you.

MARY

You are perverse.

KENNEDY

You can't know the grace which emanates from your sad, dark eyes; you can't know the sweetness which flows out of your wracked body ...

MARY

A wracked body ... what can be beautiful in that?

KENNEDY

I drink in your image every day ... the pieces of you I find on the silver tray in the morning ...

MARY

My destiny is to provoke passionate immature love, inauspicious love ... painful and misguided. Like Riccio, Riccio with his frog's eyes ... with his large head and short legs, ridiculous and generous ... he loved me like you, in an exaggerated and sensless way ... I'll never forget how he grasped my skirts screaming: *Madame, sauvez-moi!* while ten cruel hands wrenched him from me ...

KENNEDY

Your husband was jealous of him ...

MARY

Jealous of what? He was always out drinking with his friends in inns, palaces and brothels, and I should have stayed alone, to fret in purdah ... with a child of six months in my belly, Kennedy, I sat in my dining room playing cards with Riccio, my secretary, the Duchess of Argyll and Mary Seton. Riccio used to let me win and I used to scold him. He would sing, I'd ask him to sing to help me forget my husband's insulting behaviour.

KENNEDY

But he was jealous ... he was jealous of whoever came near you ...

MARY

And do you think it was out of jealousy that he made a pact with the other nobles to kill Riccio in my presence? ... how he screamed, Kennedy, when they took him into the next room ... fifty six knife wounds Kennedy ...

Striking knife blows at an imaginary body.

This for the Queen's kindness! This for your shit-face! This for your presumptuous Italian-straw eyes! This for your ill-used songs! This for the card-games you played in the Queen's apartments! This for being a presumptious bourgeois! This for believing you had won-over the nobility of Scotland! This for you, for you, for you, for you!

KENNEDY

He wanted to become king in your place ...

MARY

Darnley, my love, you didn't really want to kill our son, did you ... you are trapped by your friends, those scheming assassins ... come to Edinburgh with me, come my treasure put on your cloak, let's go ... And he came, Kennedy, he forgot all about them, he followed me docile as a lamb. He was afraid of his accomplices ...

KENNEDY

In fact they betrayed him and killed him in their turn ...

MARY

Take the baby, Kennedy ... take him to his crib ... my chest hurts ... have you seen how many bandages the doctor has tied round me to turn the milk back. But wouldn't it be better doctor if I fed him myself? ... these pains are killing me ... No, Your Majesty, your milk is watery, the little one will be fed at Lady Mary's breast, it has been decided by Parliament ... and he will be taken to Stirling Castle where the climate is more healthy ... I have forgiven you Henry for the assassination of Riccio, but I will never forget! ... now I know what stuff you are made of, you married me out of vanity, out of vanity you wanted a son, out of vanity you beat me and out of vanity you want the crown ...

ELIZABETH

Dressed all in black wearing a veil.

What happened on St. Bartholomew's night, wounds and offends me as a queen and as a Protestant. Tell your king that we are angry and grieved ... ten thousand Huguenots who had gathered in Paris to celebrate the wedding of Marguerite de Valois and Henry of Navarre ... all slain ... It is enough to declare a war ... but I will not because my country does not want war, because the principle of revenge is not mine, because we need a friend in France to counter a Spain at arms ...

Enter Nanny.

ELIZABETH

Bitch, ugly pig, cursed bitch, apeface, snake-eye ... I took you away from your father's house where you were a prisoner ... I gave you honour, riches, liberty, and you ... bitch, ugly bitch! Spuh!

Spits.

NANNY

Forgive me, Your Majesty, although I don't know what I've done, I ask your forgiveness.

ELIZABETH

Who gave you permission to marry?

NANNY

You, Your Majesty.

ELIZABETH

I ... I ... and why did you obey me, cretin?

NANNY

You advised me to marry Major Dexter and I did, even though I don't love him ... because I want children ....

ELIZABETH

You don't think of anything else, you women ... marriage, children ... at any cost ... whatever humiliation ... you want to roll yourself in the slime of humiliation, you want to be beaten, ordered about, treated badly ... the more they knock you about the more you offer your body ... cowering, sentimental, smiling, innocent, stupid, perverse, ready for any sacrifice, for any degradation ... bitch, foul horrible bitch, can't you see how your breasts sag craving to give milk ... they touch the earth and drag themselves swollen and painful ... your sensuous mouth craving to be kissed against your will, against your pride ... your cunt, silent, ready to be ripped to let out the head of an angry son who will then kick you in the arse ... don't you see how you are prostrate, ready to be bound, mounted, squeezed to the last drop of your blood after which you will be cast aside, cast aside ... go, stinking bitch and never let me see you again! You have sold your virginity, your privacy, your pride, for a foolish desire, to get in the family way.

NANNY

It was you who gave me the dowry ...

ELIZABETH

And with it you reward the hands that shackle you! Imbecile? It's better to die a hundred times than to marry!

ACT II

Mary is sleeping. Kennedy enters.

KENNEDY

I have the honour to announce that Elizabeth Queen of England wishes to see you.

MARY

Are you serious, Kennedy?

KENNEDY

She has asked that you wear a white smock as a sign of contrition ...

MARY

The Queen of Scots wear a white smock?

KENNEDY

She also asks that you put a foot on your head ...

MARY

A foot, Kennedy ... A foot?

KENNEDY

A foot, even if it be only a chicken's foot, it doesn't matter ... that is her command.

MARY

A queen with a foot on her head, it's not ... it's not right.

KENNEDY

You must also be barefoot ...

MARY

Kennedy ... what tyranny this is ...

KENNEDY

Would you like me to tell her that you refuse to see her?

MARY

No ... wait ... alright, I'll do as she wants ... I want to see her so much ... quick, Kennedy, find me a white smock and a chicken's foot ...

Kennedy takes off Mary's shoes, and puts on the smock, then leaves, while Mary puts the foot on her head. Sound of drums.

MARY

Oh God ... it's her ... how should I greet her? ... Oh Lord, help me to keep calm ...

Enter Elizabeth, richly dressed wearing her crown.

ELIZABETH

Who is that woman?

MARY

The Queen of Scots, your cousin ...

ELIZABETH

What's this – my Lords? You had told me that she was an unhappy woman prostrated by misfortune and instead I find a proud woman whose sorrows have not even bent her.

MARY

Farewell forever vain pride. I must forget who I am ... Sister, your head is happily crowned ... I worship that God whose will it was to raise you up.

ELIZABETH

What do you want, Mary Stuart? I am only here as the result of a generous impulse to which I yielded, and many people have reproached me for it ... but I have not forgotten that you tried to have me assassinated ...

MARY

I came to you as a postulant, a supplicant, and you, trampling on the laws of hospitality, had me locked up within these walls, and took my servants from me, and my friends ... but now tell me ... now tell me sincerely, of what do you accuse me?

ELIZABETH

Ever since you were in France, you laid claim to my throne, and even here, in my own backyard, you fed the flames of revolt against me.

MARY

Do not abuse your power, Cousin ...

ELIZABETH

And who would stop me? Your uncle de Guise in France, has set an example to all the world's kings, of how to make peace with one's enemies. St. Bartholomew's night shall be my lesson. What are ties of blood now? The church itself has dissolved the bonds between us by sanctifying betrayal and regicide itself. I'm simply putting into practice what your priests teach.

MARY

If you'd have recognized me as your heir, you'd have had in me a faithful and devoted cousin.

ELIZABETH

I recognize you as my heir? You, the friend of the nuns and the Pope ...

MARY

I ask you for nothing more than my life ...

ELIZABETH

Shitty slavery to govern ... stupid stinking slavery ... always having to consider public opinion in order to earn the approval of the masses. Can you really call someone a king who has to please everybody all the time? It is my virtue in this which forces me to commit this crime. We have the same blood in our veins, we are both women ... and now that I have seen you with my own eyes, swollen, old, tired, bereft of all ambition, wanting peace ... Sister, you have touched my heart ... if you renounce your claim, if you swear upon your conscience that you will no longer plot against me, I will set you free ... I will take my royal foot off your head and declare you free ...

MARY

Do you really mean that, Sister?

ELIZABETH

I have always wanted to know you ... ever since I was a child and I heard talk of your beautiful red hair, your slender body, of how you spoke Scots with a French accent ...

MARY

And I you know ... I have almost worshiped you ... I have written you ten thousand letters ... I'd have given my life to see you ... ask Kennedy, my prison companion ... if I haven't waited day after day for some sign of affection from you ...

ELIZABETH

I wear that heart-shaped diamond you gave me round my neck. I never take it off.

MARY

And I wear that enamelled ring with your initials engraved on it, on my finger ...

ELIZABETH

I was even jealous, you know, when Leicester fell in love with you from a distance ...

MARY

Years ago it was you who suggested him as a husband for me ...

ELIZABETH

It was a way of having you near me ... making you part of the most dear thing I possessed ... anyway he's a pig.

MARY

Ah! so you thought you'd give me to a pig.

Laughs.

ELIZABETH

Yes, a beautiful pig dressed up in satin and velvet!

Laughs.

MARY

A pig with a piggy soul.

ELIZABETH

A pig with piggy trotters.

MARY

A pig with piggy eyes.

ELIZABETH

A pig with a piggy face.

They laugh together. They embrace. They kiss. They dance. Mary is left alone.

MARY

Singing.

I loved a pig
With plumed hat
More handsome than Apollo.
Oh my! how did he dance!
Oh my! how did he dance!
I loved a pig,

With gryphon's face
Who used to love to hunt
Beneath my skirts so red
Beneath my skirts so red.

Kennedy enters.

KENNEDY

My lady ... wake up ... it's time for Paulet's visit.

MARY

Oh Kennedy, I was having such a beautiful dream ...

KENNEDY

Would you like a mint tisane?

MARY

I was dreaming that Elizabeth and I ... are you sure there isn't a letter for me?

KENNEDY

No letters.

MARY

I'll send her a present this evening ... all I possess now is this gold ring from my mother, Mary of Guise, I've never been without it ... I'll send it to her with one of my letters ... how gentle she was, Kennedy, how sweet my sister was!

* * *

87

ELIZABETH

I declare this sitting open! I have been reproached for having called both Houses together today, the Lords and the Commons. I have been reproached for granting this privilege to the bourgeoisie, the merchants and the squires ... so what? I am not ashamed of having called the Commons, they have been silent and absent for too long. Our Lords are often wrongfully intolerant. If they knew as I do what goes on in our country they would know how much our economy depends on the bourgeoisie, how much they have done for the good of the nation. At the death of Mary Tudor, England was in great debt, on the brink of bankruptcy, on the verge of civil war, and everybody was acting in their own interests, there are so many of these self interested people in this country ... the bourgeoisie has been faithful to the Crown and the Reform whilst many of the aristocracy have kept their connections with the French Catholics ... they were united when the great families were butchering one another, they worked on, humbly, trusting their sovereign and her politics of peace against all the warmongers then surrounding us and who still surround us ... They supported me when I wanted to reform the stale old laws relating to the estates of the church, the misused rights of the aristocracy, direct taxation ... they were with me when I decided to liberalize trade, build new ships, look for raw materials and new markets in the lands across the ocean ... finally, they helped me wipe out the nation's debts by making loans on the smallest interest ... they have shown themselves to be wise, respectful, intelligent, with that indigenous intelligence which keeps a country together. Therefore I decree that as from today they will vote in Parliament on an equal footing with the Lords ... It's no use bellowing, looking scandalized, angry ... I can see your face Lord Hamilton, it's filled with indignation and horror. You are as red as a beetroot ... bring him some vinegar and water! Steel yourself, Lord Hamilton, there's more: As from today direct taxation will be increased and the indirect taxes which affect people who can least afford them will be decreased. Those who own more and have a large income will be taxed more, while those who own nothing and have small incomes will be freed from a number of taxes ... As far as my marriage is concerned, for those of you who consider it unbecoming for a single woman to devote herself to the kingdom ... I wish to say that I consider my only husband and consort to be the kingdom of England ... and my children all the subjects of this kingdom ... However, to show my goodwill, I will consider any suitor who is put forward, always taking into account the interests of my country. But it may be, it may be that I might not choose any of them. In which case I would like written on my tomb: Here lie the bones of England's virgin Queen ... The session is closed!

* * *

MARY

Yes, Reverend Knox ... yes, I sent for you, I want to talk to you.

Imitating Knox.

— I am here as a citizen and not as a man of religion. As a citizen I must obey you. As a man of religion I must not.
— I know that you preach against me.
— Against your heresy.
— As far as I am concerned, you are the heretic. It all depends on one's point of view.
— This country has chosen the reformed religion, Your Majesty.
— And I have respected its choice.
— It has now come to the point when it is your duty, as a woman, to sensibly resign. The Crown does not become a woman.
— I've read your pamphlet, Reverend Knox ... 'First Blast of the Trumpet against the Monstrous Regiment of Women' ... What is it that makes you resent the government of a woman so much?

— If you are wise, as I believe you are, I advise you to abdicate and hand the crown over to a strong, responsible man ...

— You perhaps ...

— I have not ambitions for myself ... I only want what's good for Scotland.

— You identify yourself a little too much with Scotland.

— It is not proper that a young woman who dances should make laws in Parliament.

— What's wrong with dancing?

— Do you know what the Flesh is? Corruption and Hell. Dancing excites the Flesh. You have brought this repugnant habit with you from France ...

— And you, who, at the age of fifty-six, married a young girl of fourteen ... wasn't that for exciting the flesh?

— I'm a man and I know what I'm doing.

— I'm a woman and I know what I'm doing.

— Too proud to be religious ... God will punish you for your pride.

— Now you are identifying yourself with God ... Knox ... don't you think you exaggerate?

— You're too impudent for a woman.

— You're too impudent for a servant of God ...

— I saw you rouse your troops in helmet and breast-plate ... I must confess it made me feel sick with anger.

— None of my six thousand men were taken ill ... however, when you took part in the assassination of Cardinal Beaton, who was torn apart by possessed beasts who called themselves Reformers, I felt sick ...

— He was a traitor, he conspired with France and slept with a concubine, the lovely Marian, everybody knew, God's punishment fell upon his head.

— I could put you in prison, Knox, for your impertinence, but I shan't ...

— The people would be against you ...

— My conscience would be against me. Now go. But remember, that with your sermons you incite hatred against me ... the day when I'm no longer here to guarantee the autonomy of Scotsmen, the English will be here as your masters ...

— Give up the crown, I advise you, for the last time, you are a woman and should think only of motherhood.

— Begin by setting a good example yourself Knox, give up your property, good Christians should submit themselves to poverty and love ... you still keep your living from the state, that is, from me.

— Give up dancing and theatre ... they are instruments of the devil ...

— And you give up your beautiful child-bride ... set a good example ... take back that poor old woman who you threw out of your house ...

92

— Death will come with his sharpened scythe, and your pearls, your lace will be snatched from you, your splendid hair, your dainty feet made for dancing ... all taken away ...

Mary alone sings and dances.

You decrepid, stupid, cold, old man ... one two ... one two ... aaand three ... one two three, one two three; Queen of Hearts and King ... one two three, one two three ... dancing is harmony Knox, dancing is delight, dancing is joy, dancing is life, dancing is Love ... and I shall dance dance dance ... one two three, toe and heel, half-turn, full turn, one two three, one two three.

* * *

ELIZABETH

Queen Mary of Scotland is about to give birth ... and you? ... everybody's obsessed with my sacred belly ... sterile, empty. My royal bed, magnificent, deserted ... my dry belly ... Your Majesty, when is the happy event? when the long-awaited marriage? ... my belly is empty like a dark, empty cave ... Your Majesty, a son for the throne, a son for the crown, a son for the country ... And me? Don't I exist? I have teeth, hands, legs, a heart, a liver ...

* * *

MARY

Who said you can transfer labour pains from one body to another ... who said so ... Medusa's head, dog's piss, snake's venom ... Mother, oh Mother, free me from this pain, it's too much for me, too monstrous, too enormous ... oh Motheeer! Rot in hell you stupid dried-up cow, where are you? They've put a girl next to me ... she says she'll bear my pain, my death ... what wretch said you can share labour pains?

* * *

ELIZABETH

Your beautiful cousin has given birth to a lovely baby ... a boy with a pear-shaped head ... when will your wedding be, Your Majesty? when will you be pregnant? As if I were one of those fat white sows that live in country ditches ... if it's infertile, have it butchered ... and I, who have spent years and years bent over books ... I have learnt Latin, Greek, French, Spanish, Italian ... I have had access to the ideas of a hundred doctors ... and I have developed a memory like a huge-winged bird ... I've learnt how to look at the stars and understand the laws of physics, of astronomy ... I've learnt mathematics, music ... all the money you have spent educating me, inconstant people ... the capital used to make a queen of me ... today you are ready to throw it into the sea all because of a king who couldn't even lift the crown, he's so delicate and soft.

* * *

MARY

Oh! mercy! I'm so ill ... is the baby alive? tell me is he alright? where are you taking him? oh! mercy! I feel as if I'm dying ... the father's not here, that imbecile Henry is out drinking in some inn, making love ... his syphilis eating him away ... alone without my mother, without my husband, without my sisters ... consumed by fever ... the baby came out shoulders first ripping my flesh ... I screamed and she screamed louder than me ... I vomited and she vomited ... you say you are taking on the Queen's pains, you are suffering on her behalf, and if death is in the cards you will die for her ... hand in hand we screamed together, the two of us ... stupid and credulous to put your faith in a pigheaded doctor ... God I'm ill ... now that the baby's born, the new king, they've all gone away with him ... they've left me alone, losing all my blood, mother save me!

* * *

ELIZABETH

Lettice Knollys, the Earl of Essex's widow ...
come forward ... how old are you?

LETTICE

Twenty-two, Your Majesty.

ELIZABETH

Twenty-two ... you say it as if it burns your
mouth. Do you know how old I am?

LETTICE

I don't know.

ELIZABETH

Forty-five ... and I'm not ashamed of it ... old
wine is better than new ... if it's good quality.
Bad wine turns sour after only a few months.

LETTICE

Yes, Your Majesty.

ELIZABETH

Obedient, polite, smiling, obsequious, modest,
ingenious, submissive ... and beautiful, you are
an ideal woman ...

LETTICE

I am an unworthy servant of God.

ELIZABETH

I'm being serious. You're beautiful like a swan with new feathers, shining the whitest white ... what's the old pig like in bed?

LETTICE

I don't understand your question, Your Majesty.

ELIZABETH

Is it true or is it not, that you've secretly married my favourite, Leicester?

LETTICE

It is true.

ELIZABETH

Without him telling me a word about it, the ungrateful pig ...

LETTICE

He didn't dare.

ELIZABETH

Don't defend him!

LETTICE

I know he wanted to tell you, but ...

ELIZABETH

How dare you marry without my consent! Do you think you can take my place in that imbecile's heart? You little angel-faced lump of shit ... I'll have you sent to the Tower, I'll have you put in irons ...

LETTICE

Don't lock me up, I beg you ... I've done nothing wrong.

ELIZABETH

Don't cry. Tears bring on my nerves. Stop this instant ... would you like some beer? Drink up, I know you're not to blame ... it will be the handsome Robert who'll end up in the Tower.

LETTICE

No, I beg you ... don't lock him up ...

ELIZABETH

So, you really are in love!

LETTICE

Lock me up, rather than lock him up!

ELIZABETH

In love with that lout ... fat, bald, with a belly ... smooth and round like a porker ... and you love him ... since when?

LETTICE

Since I first met him.

ELIZABETH

Well, if you'd known him when I knew him,
when he was twenty years younger, without that
belly, with thick fair hair, strong teeth, soft eyes
... but perhaps you wouldn't have even looked at
him ... he wasn't the Queen's favourite then ...
But now, even though he's bald, plump, with
rotten teeth ... you find the Queen's favourite
desirable.

LETTICE

We love each other very much.

ELIZABETH

Ah, you love each other very much! ... and who
gave you permission to love each other very
much?

LETTICE

Love has nothing to do with permission.

ELIZABETH

Well, these are the new ideas of the young: love
has nothing to do with permission, it's unex-
pected, irrational, unstoppable, explosive ... and
every-body must bow down before its magical
power, even the Queen of England, that ugly old

virgin who doesn't know what an embrace is, doesn't know what love is, secrecy, the whispering of sweet nothings, hands in hands, kisses ...

LETTICE

As soon as we saw each other we were in love, it was fate ...

ELIZABETH

The fate of the prick!

LETTICE

I beg you not to embarrass me with language unfit for a virgin's ears.

ELIZABETH

Am I not a virgin too? But surely you know what a prick is, also called member, also called tool, also called cock? Weapon? Dick? Dong? Prong? Stonker? Shafter? Willy? Wanger? Worm? Wick? Weiner? Salami? Meat? Thing? John Thomas? John Thursday? Rod? Pee Pee Stick? No, you really don't know.

LETTICE

But our union has been blessed with the sacrament of marriage.

ELIZABETH

And what do you think marriage is? An act of sale, a contract in which you give your body, your freedom, your honour, your autonomy, your pride, your personality in exchange for a bowl of soup – in your case it will be a plate of pheasants – a roof over your head and slavery for life.

LETTICE

I love him, Ma'am.

ELIZABETH

Love will leave you, my simpleton, when you've smelt his breath for the hundredth time, when he's just woken up, when you know each hair on his legs by heart, when the stench of his sweat has clung to your nostrils ... I loved him soberly, without moons and stars on my brain. I loved him in full daylight, knowing what his soul was made of; cowardly, fatuous, feeble, smiling ... knowing what his body was made of; splendid but fragile, needing to get dressed up to make an appearance ... to make an appearance in court, in the wedding bed, in church, at war ... his appearance is simply ingratiating, it's already on the decline ...

LETTICE

Rather than know that he's locked in the Tower I swear I'll renounce my marriage ... that God might keep him safe and sound ... I ask for nothing but his freedom.

ELIZABETH

Idiot, beast, imbecile! If I separated you, your pathetic love would grow a hundred times stronger ... I would feed it, give it life ... the best way to extinguish it is to make you stay together day and night, never leaving one another. Now go ... perhaps one day, when you're tired of him, we'll be friends ... I'll tell you a few things about the man you love that will make you die laughing ... not now ... not now ... you wouldn't laugh at all now ... when you find yourself freed from this ill-considered, shameless sentiment come and see me ... goodbye, Lettice, lovely swan, be happy ... naturally you won't set foot in the Court again, I don't want to be made a fool of ... as far as your husband's concerned I know how to re-pay his betrayal.

> *She approaches Lettice, she puts a necklace round her neck and kisses her on the mouth. Then she lets her go.*

* * *

MARY

Why are you taking the reins of my horse? Why are we going to Stirling Castle by ourselves? Why are you leading me like a prisoner?

Rape, Kennedy, rape, pre-meditated in cold blood to force me to marry him ... you won't be able to undo it afterwards ... you know we love each other ... how do we love each other? I'm raping you out of love, my love ... How out of love? my body hid itself away somewhere, disgusted ... since then, Kennedy, since then, however much I looked for it, called it, I've never been able to find it again ... I wish to report to the Council of State, that the Earl of Bothwell took possession of the Queen, carried her off to Stirling Castle and raped her ... Craig, what are you saying, you criminal, I'll cut off your head, I'll slice you up like pork! 'I lay to his charge the law of adultery, he's still married to Lady Jane Gordon' ... Lady Jane who he loves more than me, Kennedy, you know as well as I do that he even wrote her a love letter from the castle when we were on our honeymoon ... I Queen Mary of Scotland place the ducal crown on Bothwell's head and create him Lord of Shetland ... he's suspected of killing your husband, Henry Lord Darnley, the Earl of Lennox, the great grandson of Henry VII of England ... three months after the death of the Queen's husband and two days after the Duke's forced divorce, Mary and Bothwell are joined together in marriage ... in the beautiful grand hall at Holyrood ... my white brocade gown ... his plumed hat ... *mense malas maio, nubere vulgus ait,* says Ovid ... only prostitutes marry in May ... how beautiful Mary our Queen was, with her hair beaded with pearls, her throat sparkling with rubies ... violet velvet, furs, a complete cask of perfumes, the horses covered in cloth of gold, her jesters in sky-blue caps ... so many gifts, Mary! I've never been so unhappy in all my life, Kennedy ... how did I come to give my body to a man who was suspected of killing my husband, in love with another woman, greedy for money and power ... how did I do it? how I did it ... so much wealth sealed with rape. Afterwards there was nothing I could do but marry him, as he said ... I knew it too ... in that rose-scented bed ... he shattered my will and then I was his, wife, lover, accomplice, prisoner, seduced and base. I'm raping you, Mary! I'm raping you out of love, happiness joy for a happy future, I'm raping you! Long live the Queen!

KENNEDY

Would you like a horseradish tisane?

MARY

Bothwell ruined me!

KENNEDY

He loved you ...

MARY

My body alienated itself so much from him that when I was pregnant it aborted by itself. I lost the child without even noticing it.

KENNEDY

He's the only one who was faithful ... when everybody was betraying you ...

MARY

If it wasn't for him I wouldn't be here now, he was my plague, my ruin ... I'm dying of him, of his delusions of grandeur, of his manic ambition ...

KENNEDY

If you want to know what people say ... they say you loved his violence like a bitch loves her master ... they say you gave up the right to govern for his beautiful male body, that you incited him to kill your husband so that you could have sex with him without hindrance and you drove him into making war with the nobility so that he might become king, the lord whose slave you were ...

MARY

Enough, Kennedy!

KENNEDY

They say he bewitched you, that he drank of your menstrual blood and with this he bound you to him forever … they say you were his whore, his prostitute, they say that in order to have him on top of you, you would have given up, not only the kingdom, the crown, but also the fruit of you belly, your son James …

MARY

Ugly sow wallowing in shit … I'll strangle you, I'll strangle you …

They scuffle. Mary throws her woman to the ground and pounds her.

Have I hurt you? Have I hurt you, tell me! Kennedy, oh God, what have I done! Kennedy, answer me! Forgive me, Kennedy, I beg you, forgive me, you know I love you, you are the only person in the world I love, apart from my son, I swear it … Kennedy, dear Kennedy, open your eyes, look at me, forgive me … I love you so much …

Mary embraces and kisses Kennedy.

* * *

ELIZABETH

'Your holiness, my father …

Reading.

who has knowledge of the human spirit'.

Commenting.

He certainly knows the shit his priests keep in their hearts well enough ...

Reading.

'My imprisonment does not prevent me from declaring myself to be a faithful subject of the church for whom I hope soon to be able to say: England is ours!'

Commenting.

A nest of vipers ... and my arse is sitting on it!

NANNY

Why don't you have her executed straight away?

ELIZABETH

Cut the head off an absolute monarch ... it's a dangerous precedent, Nanny ... and what if the unstrained mob, should call for my head tomorrow? Monarchs are and should remain untouchable, they are protected by Divine Right.

NANNY

But the Stuart woman continues to plot against you ... she escaped from Lochleven dressed as a man; she escaped from Tutbury ... now she'll escape from Fotheringhay ...

ELIZABETH

I have great faith in Paulet. She won't escape. She's guarded by three hundred men ...

NANNY

But what if she does escape, all the same? ... you know how she fascinates people, she knows how to corrupt them with pity and love ... she'll set the northern Catholics against you; she'll ask for help from Spain and France ... we'll have the enemy in our own backyard ... the Pope will lick his chops and we'll return to the black days of Mary Tudor ... Protestants at the stake and Catholics in power ...

ELIZABETH

She wouldn't succeed. The English people have had enough of priests and popes.

NANNY

I can see her now, with bare neck, hands tied behind her back, choking with anger ...

ELIZABETH

Blood disgusts me, Nanny ...

NANNY

What about all those poor people who are killed for debt, theft, conspiracy, you don't care about them being hacked to pieces.

ELIZABETH

I don't like the spectacle they make of these executions ... all these people who enjoy watching the executioner pitilessly cut, quarter and castrate ... one could say they find it pleasurable ... like eating sugar ...

NANNY

Why deny the taste for revenge? ... As a child I used to go to public executions with my grand-parents ... for me the flavour of gingerbread, vanilla, beer were all one with the sight of a naked white body which suddenly became red with blood ... God's punishment ... the first blow was a thunderbolt from heaven ... and everybody held their breath for a moment, stopped eating their fried fish and black pudding to watch, eyes popping out of their heads, to see how the naked body would react to the first blow of the hatchet ... the executioner's skill lay in the way he could open the chest and take out the heart with one movement of his wrist ... when he lifted it up to the crowd, they would applaud wildly and then set about eating and drinking again ...

ELIZABETH

'There be some sports are painful, and their labour delight in them sets off: some kinds of baseness are nobly undergone; and most poor matters point to rich gods.' My friend Shakespeare.

NANNY

You can't take these pleasures away from the people.

ELIZABETH

Last night I dreamt that I embraced her ... I kissed her ... I gave her permission to go to France ... she's a poor woman with swollen legs and sick eyes ...

NANNY

But she constantly plots against you ... you forget the carter.

ELIZABETH

That is one of Walsingham's infamies ... he has procured false friends for her, false admirers, false spies. And this carter who carried her messages in his barrels ... all controlled by him, plotted by him ...

NANNY

Just as you wanted ...

ELIZABETH

I have accepted the counsels of the secret services. As is befitting a queen ... but how disgusting
Nanny ... those sickening lies I'm obliged to sign
for 'the good of the state' ... I am vindictive, as
you know, if someone offends against me, I kill
them ... but these atrocious plots of the secret
services make my stomach turn ... bought
testimonies made in cold blood ... I want to be
a lion not a rat.

NANNY

Now, you have proof of her desire to kill you
and take your place.

ELIZABETH

There will be a trial. Babington is compromised
up to his neck, he will be executed and Gifford
too ... they fell into the trap like rabbits
disemboweled with their eyes open and cut
into pieces ... that is their fate ... I will ask for
them to be quartered after they are dead ... but
I don't know if I'll get that. My subjects are very
exacting on the subject of spectacle.

NANNY

She should be the first to die ...

ELIZABETH

Mary isn't stupid ... she never signed anything ... she can say that she didn't write those letters ...

MARY

Here I am, in front of you my lords, judges ... you didn't want me to have a seat and that's fine, I'll make the best of it, though I'm not steady on my feet ... you didn't want to give me a lawyer in my defence ... and that's fine, I'll make the best of it, I will defend myself ... First of all, I declare that as sovereign of a foreign country you do not have the right to try me for treason. I have no obligation of fealty to a queen who imprisoned me when I had only asked for refuge.

As an absolute sovereign, I cannot submit myself to orders, nor can I submit myself to the laws of a foreign country, without suffering insult to myself, to the King my son, and to my people ... I do not recognize the laws of England. I declare that, with every right, I requested the aid of the sovereigns of France, my relations, those of Spain, my relations, in order to help deliver me from this unworthy imprisonment ... But I swear that I have never been involved in plots against the life of Elizabeth, my cousin in flesh ... My claims to the English throne are more than legitimate, and you all know it. As far as descent is concerned,

I am the closest to the Crown. But I have never wanted to take the Crown from her head. What I asked for, was the right of succession. But Elizabeth, preoccupied with questions of religion, has never wanted to concede it to me. Well, I sought to have this recognition all the same, that was part of my privilege as a sovereign. I do not consider that I have done anything dishonest. It is the right of every innocent prisoner to try, in every way, to escape and restore their honour ... and therefore, I ask you to treat me as a queen with due honour. I do not ask for mercy, but for worthy treatment. I am afraid of being poisoned, liquidated. For days I have not tasted the food in my prison. If you wish to condemn me to death, do so, but as a queen, not as a criminal, for I am a queen and not a criminal!

* * *

ELIZABETH

It is intolerable that during my lifetime I must stand before my shroud. Do you think that I can love my shroud? Tell my royal sister that our two religions are mortal enemies. It is insupportable that the Reformed Church should be replaced by Catholicism through the right of succession. History asks for a choice: me or her. Lay government or Catholic government. It is not for me, but for the English people to choose.

* * *

MARY

Bring me a tisane, Kennedy, of dragon's blood ... my head aches, and standing up for so many hours ...

KENNEDY

They've got your letters. They'll sentence you to death.

MARY

That's what I want. I'm tired of living.

KENNEDY

Only two years ago you were racing on horseback like an amazon. You remember when we escaped from Lochleven ... two days gallop in the rain ...

MARY

Now my legs are swollen with rheumatism, my head is heavy, my eyes hurt ... being locked up without being able to move about has killed me. I'm already dead. My execution will only be the severing of my last tired threads. Kennedy, I'll come and find you in your dreams sometimes, don't chase me away.

KENNEDY

Mortimer has been stabbed to death. Babington has been killed. Douglas has been quartered, Gifford disemboweled ... and the stupid Earl of Leicester is locked in the Tower, though I don't know whether it's because he tried to help you, or because he married the lovely Lady Lettice Essex in secret.

MARY

The only thing I want, Kennedy, is to see my son again ... who knows how much suffering my fate must be causing him.

KENNEDY

Your son is very well. He doesn't suffer at all. He even declined to ask for mercy on your behalf, so as not to quarrel with Elizabeth, who's given him a good deal of money and soldiers in order to keep the Catholic provinces quiet ... he has renounced your religion. Perhaps he will obtain the longed-for succession to the English throne, he's become a Protestant for this reason ... he's much more cunning than you, your son.

MARY

Has no-one done anything for me?

KENNEDY

Henry of France your brother-in-law. But the only response was that he should mind his own business.

MARY

Writing.

'Dear cousin and sister ... there was a time when it was said: if one of us were a man our marriage would be the most sensible in history ... I would have married you willingly, if that could have been today, we would be happy having united England and Scotland in a knot of love and concord' ... Kennedy, I think I'm becoming sentimental, old and sentimental ... if Scotland wanted to remain Catholic, such a marriage would be my ruin ... my grandmother Antoinette de Guise said: 'Rather than whine bite your tongue with your teeth' ... 'Dear Sister, as you live in glory and I am about to die, I ask you as Queen and as my cousin to send my body to France, to free my servants, to send my son James, King of Scotland, this last memory of the Guise family, Catholic and faithful to the Pope, to let my confessor say a public mass in my name ... Europe is about to watch you. Behave justly! your little loved but very loving cousin Mary Stuart' ... There, seal my letter with Span-ish wax, wrap it in white silk and hand it over to my wretched jailor Mr. Paulet, and beg him to forward it as quickly as possible.

* * *

ELIZABETH

Will no-one free me from my duty as executioner? Paulet, I handed the Queen over to you as the most precious thing in the world ... you have guarded her most conscientiously! Sometimes queens are not taken at their word, Paulet! you should have thought to rid me of the weight of this terrible decision. Isn't poison preferable to a public execution? 'I hope never to see the day when my queen should ask me to perform an act which is forbidden both by God and the law' ... What a noble reply! Mr. Paulet declines to dirty his hands! But he didn't turn up his nose when he was asked to be a jailor in my pay ... (and when he participated in Walsin-gham's ignoble schemings, to pay spies, traitors, he didn't turn his head). A secret and decisive act at this time would save England from the condemnation of the Pope, and an attack from Henry of France and perhaps even a religious war! the people want her head, Paulet, and I have a duty to condemn her, but at the same time, if I condemn her I am lost ...

* * *

MARY

Why are you crying, Kennedy? ... it won't be my death you'll be witnessing but my triumph. Now listen: these are the few things I have left. To Gertrude who is young and has yet to marry I leave my damask gown, to Rosamund who everybody calls moonfish because of her fat ugly face, I leave these two pearls that I wear in my ears so that she will shine more brightly ... to my faithful Maurice, I leave this silver box ; to sweet Burgoing I'll give my lute so he will remember the many sad evenings when we consoled ourselves with music; to Elizabeth, my cook, who has a baby at her breast, I'll give this miniature of my new-born son so she might learn that children grow up to become enemies; to you, I leave this medallion with the portrait of my mother, the person who was most dear to me in the world so that you'll remember that ties between women are the strongest and most lasting ... take this white silk handkerchief which I embroidered ... I want to be blindfold with this when the time comes. I want you to do me this last service.

KENNEDY

The Sheriff won't let me accompany you to the scaffold.

MARY

What? They want to deny me thi~~small~~ ... mall
favour?

KENNEDY

He says that women weep on the scaff~~ol~~
confusion, disturb the executioner ... ~~e~~

MARY

I'll vouch for you, I'll tell him that yc
weep. I know your strength of spirit. I ~~w~~
to be with me, Kennedy, you carried me
arms when I was small, your hand must g~~u~~
at the time of my death ...

KENNEDY

Leicester is outside waiting to take you t~~c~~
scaffold. Elizabeth has charged him to att~~e~~
your death to punish him for having tried to ~~s~~
you free.

MARY

Lord Leicester, you have kept your word ... you
promised me your arm to take me out of prison
and here you are, punctually. You planned to set
me free and marry me and become King since
our dear sister had rejected you ... today you are
accompanying me to the scaffold instead of the
altar ... you sought the hearts of two queens with

y and thoughtlessness of a vain old man
th ppy if you can ... adieu!

*Music and drums. Mary dressed all in red
goes away towards the axe.*

* * *

KENNEDY

Queen has gone into the death-chamber ...
iundred lords are sitting around the catafal-
ie which rises, black, in front of the furthest
all. The executioner, Mr. Bull, tells her to take
)ff her jacket in order to expose her neck. My
Queen takes off her jacket ... she is left in a full
skirt and a crimson bodice embroidered with
pearls. Now her neck is completely bare. The
executioner Mr. Bull puts his hands on her
golden rosary to take it away, as is usual with
those condemned to death, but Mary stops him
with these words: executioner, you will be rec-
ompensed in money, but let this rosary be, it is
for my confessor, Monsieur de Preau, so that it
can be taken to France as a last memento of
me ...

The Dean of Peterborough asks her to convert
to the Reformed Church before her execution.
The Queen answers, 'No; if I should convert
now, in the face of death, I would be despicable,
not Protestant. I remain faithful to the religion

of my birth.' The executioner, Mr. Bull, makes to tie a black cloth around the Queen's head. She stops him with a decisive gesture. Straight away, I bring the silk handkerchief, embroidered by her with golden doves and I fasten it round her temples. She thanks me by squeezing my wrist. Now Bull's assistant Mr. Craig puts his gloved hands upon the Queen's body to hold her still. Mary protests that there's no need, she swears that she'll stay still. But Mr. Craig continues to hold her and answers with these words: 'Your body can move against your will, madam.'

Now the executioner, Mr. Bull, lets fall the first blow of the axe. But it misses her neck and hits the back of her head, chipping a piece of it off.

My Queen murmurs 'Sweet Jesus' whilst her body gives a sudden tremor.

Bull lets fall a second blow and succeeds in severing the head from the neck. But two sinews remain attached. Bull takes a saw and finishes his work ...

Meanwhile my Queen's lips are still moving. Bull lifts up the head to show it to the public. As he raises his arm her head falls to the ground. Between his fingers he is holding thick chestnut locks tinged with red. My Queen's head lies on the ground, her hair closed-cropped and grey.

Now the Dean of Peterborough stands up and shouts out: 'So perish all the Queen's enemies!

'The others shout back in chorous: 'Long live the Queen!'

The embalmers have come to take the body ... but there's something moving under my queen's skirts: her little Skye terrier comes out terror-striken and starts whining by her mistress' hand. Today, Wednesday 8th February, 1587 at ten o'clock in the morning, Queen Mary Stuart, in her forty-fourth year, is no more.

Do not weep for her death
Rejoice in her tranquillity
The bud opened to let out the flower
The chains broken to free the prisoner
The star of her name is burnt out
Now she will journey in the snow-white silence
    of the eternal dream.

END

On next page: Jennifer Hurd and Elicia Young in Mary Stuart. *Directed by Rhoda Helfman Kaufman, California State University, Hayward, 1990. Photo credit: Tony Chilimidos.*

Dialogue Between a Prostitute and Her Client

Translated by Tony Mitchell

Preface

For Maraini, prostitution is a metaphor. Historically, women have traded their bodies for money, protection, or security. To this day, girls are educated to use their bodies to gain favor, acceptance, a partner, a job, or whatever else they want. Manila, the prostitute in this play, is not a victim of circumstance. She is well-educated, and aware of what she is doing. She decides to sell herself; it is a political decision. 'The only choice a woman's got is whether she prostitutes herself in public or in private – on the street or at home,' Manila says in the play.

Prostitution is portrayed here 'as an occupation with no more rewards than many others.' In fact, this prostitute serves a 'proletarian social service through which many males suffering from *mammismo* (dependence on the mother) are counseled ... [This] can serve to prevent sexual violence.' *

The play's structure allows direct confrontation between audience and actors. Manila speaks to the audience, asking questions such as

---

* Tony Mitchell, 'Scrittura femminile: Writing the Female in the Plays of Dacia Maraini', *Theatre Journal*, v. 42, n°. 3, p. 332-349, at p. 341

'Which part [of the female body] do you prefer? Breasts? Thighs?' and 'Are you an expert on prostitutes? Have you ever been to one?'

The character of Manila the prostitute is a complex one. She derives sexual pleasure from her encounter with the client, but she translates that into a maternal nurturing impulse. She also craves affection. Her rich sensory imagination allows her to fall so far into the selves of others that she identifies with them and loses her very self.

The play explores the dynamics of seduction while reversing the conventions of bedroom comedy. 'You're really helping yourself through me,' Manila tells the Client, and it is he (not she) who appears naked on the stage.

Dialogue was performed in English in London, England by the Monstrous Regiment Company in 1980, and in Sydney, Australia in 1988. The translation presented here, by the Australian Tony Mitchell, was used in the Sydney performance directed by Franco Cavarra, with Carmelina Di Guglielmo as Manila and Stephen Hutchison as the Client. The British production was directed by Ann Mitchell, with Chris Bowler as Manila and John Slade as the Client, translation by Gillian Hanna. The play has also been performed in Austria, Belgium, Brazil, France, Germany, Italy, and Portugal.

Dialogue Between
a Prostitute and Her Client

Characters

Manila

Client

MANILA

Well, are you going to take your clothes off?

CLIENT

What do you think I am, a woman?

MANILA

No, I can see you've got a dick.

CLIENT

And what the hell are you?

MANILA

I'm wearing a skirt, aren't I?

CLIENT

You're not one of those transvestites are you? Look, I don't go with guys.

MANILA

Don't be silly. I'm a woman.

CLIENT

Women don't behave like that.

MANILA

How do they behave?

CLIENT

I don't know … they flirt more – wiggle their ass – play up to you.

MANILA

I am not a dog. Take your clothes off.

CLIENT

Is this some sort of put-down?

MANILA

Take your shirt off so I can have a good look at you.

CLIENT

What's there to see?

MANILA

I want to see what your chest's like.

CLIENT

Sorry, but I'm the one who's doing the buying, not you.

MANILA

I realize you're the customer, but I'd like to have a look at what I'm getting. I'm a voyeur. Let me see your chest.

CLIENT

There's nothing special about my chest. I never went in for sports. My mother wanted me to row on a crew team, but I never got into it. Pellizetti reckons you can find more homosexuality in male team sports than in a bar full of screaming queens.

MANILA

Who's Pellizetti?

CLIENT

You've never heard of Pellizetti? No, of course not – you're just a pro.

MANILA

Why have you still got your clothes on?

CLIENT

What sort of woman are you?

MANILA

This isn't an interrogation. You're buying. I'm selling. It's strictly business.

CLIENT

Right. And the deal is I take and you get taken.

MANILA

Oh no, you don't. You're buying and I'm selling. That's all there is to it.

CLIENT

What are you selling?

MANILA

My cunt.

CLIENT

Don't say that word please.

MANILA

Why not? Does it disgust you?

CLIENT

Look, just don't say it when I'm around. It's gross. It shows a lack of respect for your own body.

MANILA

What's the matter? This is strictly business, right?

CLIENT

Sure, but if you don't keep up your end of the deal I'll get turned off. I'll lose my desire ...

Pause. Manila watches the client. He puts his handkerchief to his temples. He's got a headache.

CLIENT

Why don't you say something?

MANILA

So you don't just want my cunt, you want conversation too? I'm not a geisha girl.

CLIENT

I already asked you not to be gross.

MANILA

Is 'cunt' gross?

CLIENT

Please don't say that word. I can't stand it.

MANILA

You can stand to buy it by the pound though.

CLIENT

Look, I'm paying ... I'm paying alot of money for this and I don't want to hear those words, OK?

MANILA

You're not paying that much. I'm selling you my body at a discount if you include use of the room, the bed, the sheets, the ashtray, the window, the toilet ...

CLIENT

God, how mercenary. All you can think of is money. Haven't you got anything inside – any emotions? Don't you ever suffer, or cry? Haven't you got a soul?

MANILA

No.

CLIENT

Bloody hell. I can't get rid of this headache.

MANILA

How old are you?

CLIENT

Twenty-five. Why?

MANILA

You sound like you're about fifty.

CLIENT

I'm burnt out. I've been on the go non-stop for about a month.

MANILA

How come?

CLIENT

It's election time. How else do you think I got the money to come here?

MANILA

Who were you campaigning for?

CLIENT

Oh, just what I needed. Talking politics with a prostitute.

MANILA

Are you a liberal?

CLIENT

If you say another word about politics I'm going.

MANILA

It's like that, is it? Do you want some coffee?

CLIENT

No, I want to rest. Is it OK if I lie down?

She watches him lie down and smoke a cigarette. To audience.

MANILA

I look at him. Look all over him. Every bit of him, head to toe. I like looking at things. I always have. I look at something, then I look again, and then suddenly I fall right into what I'm looking at. It's dangerous – looking gives me a jolt, like cold water on my back. If I go on looking after a certain point I just throw myself right into whatever it is I'm looking at, and I'm not there anymore. I fall right to the bottom and sink. Then I start swimming, running, spreading out. I say to myself, I'm me, Manila, don't worry. But it's not me at all. I've turned into the thing I'm looking at. A dog for example. A dog crapping on the pavement; the turd won't come out of its ass. Its owner is pulling on the leash and nearly choking it, the idiot's ashamed of his dog being seen shitting against the corner shop. A soft yellow turd – must have a bad liver. It's owner probably hasn't got time to look after it properly – too lazy, sleeps in the mornings, and feeds the dog any old rubbish, so it gets sick. So here's this dog – or Manila who's become the dog – trapped with its hind leg stuck up in the air, its ass straining, head looking up at the man saying, 'Hang on, master, can't you see I'm trying to shit?'

Pause. The client hasn't heard anything. He moves.

CLIENT

This silence is getting on my nerves. What are you doing? Are you asleep?

MANILA

No. You were asleep.

CLIENT

You're not a prostitute. I'm an expert. You're something else. A nut case, some sort of pervert, or an actress. You're just playing games. I don't know. Anyway you're not what I'm paying to fuck.

First interruption and debate with the audience.

MANILA

Shut up.

CLIENT

Prompting her.

What the hell do you want ...

MANILA

I know what my next line is. I was just thinking about the word 'prostitute'. What does being an 'expert on prostitutes' mean?

To a man in the audience.

Are you an expert on prostitutes? Have you ever been to one? Would you say a prostitute behaves in a particular kind of way? If so, how?

The discussion goes on as long as the audience respond. Then the actors go back to the script.

CLIENT

You're not a prostitute. I'm an expert.

MANILA

What the hell do you want? And take off that shirt.

CLIENT

Anyone'd think you were buying and I was selling. You're starting to get on my nerves.

MANILA

Right. You say what you want and we'll do it.

CLIENT

Let's pretend I picked you up on a bus, and you're not sure if you should be unfaithful to your husband or not.

MANILA

That's no good. I haven't got a husband anyway.

CLIENT

You can pretend.

MANILA

So I have to be an actor now too?

CLIENT

It's got nothing to do with acting. Just do what I say.

MANILA

I don't do acting. I just sell cunt.

CLIENT

Would you stop saying that word? Goddamn prostitute. You're spoiling everything.

MANILA

You've got lovely green eyes. Or are they blue?

CLIENT

Really? You think so?

MANILA

You're a bit skinny though. Let's see your hands.

CLIENT

You're screwing it all up.

MANILA

Very nice. You obviously don't work with hands like these. You must work with your head. Is that why you've got a headache?

CLIENT

My work needs brains and brawn. And guts.

MANILA

Nice mouth too.

CLIENT

That's what they all say.

MANILA

Give us a smile ... nice teeth too.

He smiles.

Smile again – you've got a nice smile. A bit moody, but nice. What's your name?

CLIENT

What's all this nice mouth stuff? Who's the customer here anyway?

MANILA

Bet you're pretty well-off, huh?

CLIENT

You don't make much out of a candy store.

MANILA

You're a shopkeeper?

CLIENT

My father is.

MANILA

And what do you do?

CLIENT

I'm a student. Business and Economics. Look, Manila. I'm not one of those macho types. If I was, I would have thrown you down on the bed by now, no messing around. I like to get to know people first. I like to have a good look at them and try to understand them. I like you to be you and me to be me. I don't get any kicks out of treating you like an animal. I believe in good manners. You might say I'm a bit of a gentleman.

MANILA

You're not a fascist, are you?

CLIENT

No, I'm not. I vote democrat. Why?

MANILA

I don't go with fascists.

CLIENT

Bit picky for a prostitute, aren't you?

MANILA

Mind your own fucking business. And take your shirt off.

CLIENT

I'm not taking anything off. God, my head. Have you got any aspirin?

MANILA

I'll have a look.

She finds some aspirin and holds the packet out to him.

CLIENT

Not like that.

MANILA

Like what?

CLIENT

In the palm of your hand. Like this. So I can pick it up with my tongue and taste your flesh. That's how my mother always does it. She always laughs when I lick her hand, and calls me her little puppy dog. Would you massage my feet, Manila?

Manila takes his feet in her hands.

MANILA

Feet can talk. They can tell you alot, feet. My grandmother used to say, always look at a man's feet. If they're too small, stay away from him. If they're too hot and clammy, stay away. If they're like two little corpses, stay away. But if they're ticklish and a bit smelly, hang on to them – they're friendly feet. Are you going to take off your shirt?

CLIENT

All right. There. What do you think?

MANILA

Not bad. A bit hairy. I don't like men with hairy
chests. I always judge a man by his chest. If it's
hairy, it means he's vain and hypocritical. Then
I look at his hips. Then his ass. The last thing I
look at is his dick. It's the least expressive part of
a man. And the most false. If you really want to
know something, dicks never tell you the truth.
When they're hard, they stick out like they want
to skewer you. But the minute you criticise
them, they shrivel up in terror like pansies. But
the shy, cute ones that are a bit clammy and give
you the impression they're having a hard time
staying up, are often the most cunning and
devious ones. They never get tired, and they're
likely to spurt seed into your belly when you
least expect it and make you pregnant before
you've got time to say 'be careful'. Then there
are the moody dicks: long and thin, and smooth
and warm. When you hold them in your hand
they feel nice and sleek, but they're real creeps,
and they're so full of themselves they'll only
stand up for you if you flatter them. Then they
go limp at the crucial moment and you spit them
out coughing. Then there are pear-shaped dicks,
thin on top and fat underneath. They're a pain

in the ass – always arguing. The base says one thing and the superstructure says another, and between the two of them they can never manage to get anything together. The spare-part dicks look like they've swallowed a broom; they're always standing at attention like soldiers. They're hopeless – they go off to war, stick their bayonets into the enemy's body and then head back to the trenches for orders. They're the worst sort – stupid ignorant dickheads. They are a real drag. Then you've got the dicklets. They flit around without a care in the world, gossiping and snooping around. They usually stink of fish and chips, and worm their way into every nook and cranny, especially mouths and butts. They like to spread themselves around, and if you don't like it they bitch and moan and wriggle around like worms. Then there's the dick that sulks if you so much as say hello to it, and the touchy type with no sense of timing, that always hangs around when its not wanted. The childish dick wants mommy to stroke it all the time. The masochistic dick turns up its nose at you and won't keep still unless you give it a whack the minute you see it. So much for the two-faced dicks who never tell the truth.

Pause. The client wakes up.

CLIENT

What are doing holding my feet?

MANILA

You said you wanted a massage.

CLIENT

I must have fallen asleep. How long have I been asleep?

MANILA

About half an hour.

CLIENT

Shit, what a waste of half an hour. We'll knock twenty dollars off the bill, eh?

MANILA

Fuck that. You might have been sleeping but I've been working.

CLIENT

On a dead man's feet?

MANILA

It's work as far as I'm concerned, feet or no feet. You pay for the use of the bed and the pillow too, you know.

CLIENT

You sound quite educated. Where do you come from?

MANILA

I've got a degree in literature and philosophy for what it's worth.

CLIENT

Christ, this bloody headache! What's a university graduate doing in a place like this? If you don't mind my asking.

MANILA

What do you think?

CLIENT

Why aren't you teaching in some school somewhere, instead of going to bed with strangers?

MANILA

Mind your own business.

CLIENT

You're really turning me off, you know, Manila. It's getting me down.

MANILA

Well, I'll get you up again in a minute, so what are you complaining about?

CLIENT

How about taking some clothes off?

MANILA

Look, you're the good-looking one. I'm a bit shop-soiled, like most consumer products, so I don't feel like stripping.

CLIENT

All right. If that's the way you want it. Would you put your hand on my forehead? You know what my mother says when I've got a temperature? 'Temperature, temperature sickness disease, Off you go home as fast as you please.'

MANILA

I bet your mother works the register.

CLIENT

How did you know?

MANILA

And at noon she goes off to cook lunch and your sister takes over.

CLIENT

My girlfriend, actually.

MANILA

Why do you have to come see me if you've got a girlfriend? Do you sleep with her?

CLIENT

Of course I do. We're not living in the Victorian age.

MANILA

So?

CLIENT

So what?

MANILA

Why do you need me to screw you?

CLIENT

You sound just like my mother. Why do you have to go with those tarts? Spending good money you should be buying furniture for your house with!

MANILA

Don't you like your girlfriend?

CLIENT

She's beautiful. She's tall, slim, blonde, delicate – I'm almost afraid to touch her. She's a qualified shorthand typist – makes good money too. And she loves me. When she comes over to my place the first thing she asks me is what I want to eat. I can take my pick from the gourmet cookbook, so I always choose the most complicated dishes

I can find and she cooks them for me. Have you ever tried truffle consume?

MANILA

What's that?

CLIENT

Truffle consume is frog's leg soup with milk, cream, peas, cinnamon, saffron, nutmeg, rolled oats and butter with grated truffles on top. My mother's really proud of her. They're always ganging up on me and spying on me. So I play tricks on them. I've got a right to be independent. And there are some things I can't do with her - she'd think they were dirty.

MANILA

For example?

CLIENT

Like holding my feet – she'd never do that.

MANILA

Are your feet dirty?

CLIENT

And my mother's always in the way. When I fuck her I feel like I'm fucking my mother.

MANILA

Do that again!

CLIENT

Do what again?

MANILA

That – raising your eyebrows. You've got lovely
eyes.

CLIENT

Look deep into my eyes and you'll see a rose
palpitating.

MANILA

Is that what your mother says?

CLIENT

Well it's true, isn't it?

MANILA

What are your girlfriend's eyes like?

CLIENT

Small and dark. She's small all over. Small teeth,
small eyes – like a pig's, small hands like a
monkey's, small feet like a mouse, small breasts
like turnips. How can a woman go around
without any breasts? Let me see your breasts,
Manila.

MANILA

Leave my breasts alone.

CLIENT

I've got a thing about breasts. They really turn me on. I can't do a thing without them.

MANILA

What do you do with them? They're only breasts.

CLIENT

I cling to them, chew them, suck them. Breasts are everything.

MANILA

Well mine are full of milk.

CLIENT

Milk? My God. Full of milk? How come?

MANILA

Because I had a baby a few months ago, idiot.

CLIENT

Oh God, I'm getting a hard-on.

MANILA

At last. Take your pants off then.

CLIENT

You're wierd, you know. You keep seeing things from my point of view, and it really turns me off. You're not normal. You keep putting me off.

MANILA

What the hell do you care if I'm normal or not?

CLIENT

Have you really got milk?

MANILA

Yes. Why?

CLIENT

You've really blown the top off my head, you know. I've had this obsession ever since I was a little kid. I used to hide in the church when it was dark so I could be alone with the statue of Mary and hold on to her breasts and cry. I used to swallow my tears and pretend they were milk flowing and flowing, and then I'd end up coming in my pants like a little fool. Would you let me do it to you?

Interruption and discussion with audience.

MANILA

This business about the milk. I hear it quite often, and I find it offensive. Apart from the fact that it makes you into a surrogate mother, it means only one particular part of your body is the object of desire, not your whole body. I bet you …

To audience.

... have favorite parts of the female body too, like a butcher's shop. A shoulder of lamb, a chicken thigh ... the female body is chopped up and idolized in pieces.

To a man in the audience.

Which part do you prefer? Breasts? Thighs?

Discussion with the audience. When it is over the client says his last line.

MANILA

What does your girlfriend think about you going to prostitutes?

CLIENT

I don't tell her about it. And don't call yourself that. Don't degrade yourself.

MANILA

What should I call myself?

CLIENT

I don't know – masseuse, escort, courtesan ... You need a bit of fantasy in your life, why don't you use your imagination? I mean, here I am in a room with a person I don't even know, with everything to discover, a whole world to invent ... Anything can happen. That's the way I see things – it's like an adventure.

MANILA

How much do you expect for the little bit you're paying me?

CLIENT

Why do you have to ruin everything?

MANILA

I don't think I could ever have an adventure with you.

CLIENT

Why not?

MANILA

Because you're as flat as an ironing board. You're a bore.

CLIENT

All you need is a bit of imagination ... If I close my eyes I can imagine you're a virgin ... a completely different sort of girl, who's lonely, who's never had a man before and won't let anyone touch her.

MANILA

You'd love to rape me, wouldn't you? I look at him. I look into the dirty dishwater of his heart. I look into those green eyes and desire creeps down my spine. A desire to get inside this student of business and economics, into his chest, his black eyelashes, his breath that smells of cigarette smoke. I almost become him.

CLIENT

You're a bit weird, aren't you Manila? A bit of a perv, eh?

MANILA

What the fuck are you talking about?

CLIENT

Don't be vulgar.

MANILA

Take off your underpants.

CLIENT

Fuck off, bitch! Who's the customer here, me or you?

MANILA

You're the one with the money, so you're the customer. But you're the only one who'll be getting any pleasure out of it, so you're really buying yourself through me.

CLIENT

You're not a prostitute. I don't know what you are, but you're not a prostitute. You're really turning me off.

MANILA

Shall we screw then?

CLIENT

No. Not like that. I need to relax. A bit of atmosphere. Would you turn on the radio?

Manila turns on the radio. Music.

CLIENT

There. Music. Soft lights, and a warm female body. What more can you ask?

MANILA

Do you want to know how many I go through in a day?

CLIENT

Shut up – you're turning me off!

MANILA

Between three and five o'clock, two. Six to eight, five. Some of them only want fifteen minutes, so they don't have to pay as much. On Saturday afternoon I went through fifteen.

CLIENT

Christ, this damn headache! Turn that cont-raption off will you.

Manila turns the radio off.

CLIENT

You ruined it. You really fucked it up. Haven't you got any sense of fantasy? To think I could come here every week for the next ten years.

MANILA

Who'd put up with you for ten years? Are you crazy?

CLIENT

Maybe not in August. I usually go to the beach with my family. But for the rest of the year. We could fix a price. Regular payments.

MANILA

You mean so much a month, like a salary?

CLIENT

My father has been going to the same prostitute for twenty five years.

MANILA

What does your mother think about that?

CLIENT

What's my mother got to do with it? She only sleeps with my father out of duty. She doesn't even know what sex is. She's never had an orgasm in her life. She's had five kids and never had an orgasm.

MANILA

How do you know?

CLIENT

Once I came home and saw her sitting on the couch in her nightie talking on the phone. The radio was on – it was one of those FM talkradio programs and she was telling them everything 'I've never had an orgasm. My husband's a pig who just gets what he wants and then rolls over and goes to sleep. My son's a disgusting selfish faggot bastard. I've been scrubbing floors for fifty years and now I don't even know who I am.' Guess what I did.

MANILA

You smashed the radio against the wall, slammed the door and ran out of the house?

CLIENT

I beat her up.

MANILA

You do look a bit like a Gestapo officer with your little blond beard and your snaky eyes.

CLIENT

What would you do? She was pouring out all her intimate secrets on the radio! I nearly strangled her.

MANILA

I bet you were sorry afterwards.

CLIENT

I felt bad when I saw her all bruised and crying.
I said I was sorry, and gave her a hug and a kiss.
She is my mother after all.

MANILA

Take off your underpants.

The client takes his underpants off.

MANILA

You've got a nice dick. A bit stupid though. It's
not one of those dicks that realizes right away
what it's supposed to do.

CLIENT

Are you insulting me now?

MANILA

Not you, just your dick.

CLIENT

We're one and the same person. It's gone down
now.

MANILA

I'll soon get it up again. That's my job, isn't it?

To the audience.

I take this piece of limp and flabby meat in my hand. There's not a drop of blood in it – it's soft and floppy like a glove. I squeeze it and knead it and pull it and stroke it and make it dance, until the beast sticks its head up and then quick as a flash I get on top of it. He's angry: who said you could get on top? You're suffocating me! I say keep still and keep quiet or we'll be in big trouble. I've worked my ass off getting you hard, and I'm on top so I can push you out when I want to so I don't get pregnant. He shifts about a bit – he's not a bad swimmer. He moves about from side to side and it's quite pleasant. But the hideous, horrible thing about it is I'm falling into this sweaty body. I hang on to the sides with my fingers, but I can't stop it. I hardly notice I'm slipping into the slimy water and turning into him – timid, gurgling, thirsting for his mother's milk. I undo my blouse and give him my milk to drink and he, or rather I, comes like a fountain, a river, a cascade, a flood. I'm a love-struck dick inside my mother's cunt and the milk I'm pouring down his thoat arouses me, churns me up and tugs at my breast until I become milk in my son's throat. I'm my son spitting his sweet seed into my belly which is his belly and I'm inside my mother and the son of the mother who is milk for my beloved maternal love.

Silence. He revives and puts his underpants back on. Then he looks in the miror.

CLIENT

Pity you're a prostitute. It doesn't suit you. Couldn't you find something better to do, like teaching or something ... working in a school? Aren't you ashamed of being so educated and doing a shitty job like this?

MANILA

Still stunned.

What?

CLIENT

A nice girl like you.

MANILA

Have you taken up preaching now?

CLIENT

In a few years no one'll want you anymore, you know. You'll be on the scrapheap, sinking lower and lower.

MANILA

What are you getting at?

CLIENT

You took something from me too, Manila. You got pleasure from me. You didn't think I noticed. Just because I didn't say anything doesn't mean I'm stupid. I noticed you were getting pleasure – so in a way our relationship's not just a financial agreement anymore.

MANILA

What exactly are you getting at? Let me get this straight. If it's not just a financial agreement anymore, what the fuck is it? A present? You think I should give your washed-out Nazi face a present?

CLIENT

You got it, Manila. I knew you were intelligent.

MANILA

Got what?

CLIENT

We're even. We're not from two opposite social classes, buying and selling. We're equal. We're both poor, and both exploited, aren't we?

MANILA

Sorry, hang on a minute, will you? Can you say that again? What the fuck are you trying to tell me?

CLIENT

I'm telling you I'm really crazy about your body
Manila. You've got a really amazing body. I'm
saying I really like making love with you, you've
got incredible breasts, your milk's really sweet,
and you like having sex with me beacuse I'm
young and good-looking and I've got a good
body. We could start getting involved and may
be in the future ...

MANILA

In other words, you're refusing to pay.

CLIENT

Why pay for something that involves giving
yourself spontaneously? This is love, Manila.
True love.

MANILA

Listen, snake-eyes. If this is your way of saying
you're not going to pay me I'll stick a knife in
your guts. Got it?

CLIENT

People don't like to use knives, or guns. We're
rational, feeling people. Like Lenin said,
discipline, work and study.

MANILA

I use knives when I have to.

CLIENT

You love me, Manila.

MANILA

I don't love you in the slightest. I couldn't give
a shit about you.

CLIENT

You do, you know. I could be the man in your
life. I could give you back the tenderness you've
lost in this shitty profession. I could be a father
to your child. What do you think?

MANILA

Get your money out.

CLIENT

You'll get your money, don't worry. Christ, I
don't believe it. You haven't understood a thing
I've said. It's not the money I'm talking about.
It's our future.

MANILA

Your future, fuckwit.

CLIENT

No. Ours. How old are you? Thirty, thirty-five?
It doesn't matter, I don't want to know. You
could be eighteen as far as I'm concerned.
We're two of a kind, Manila. We both like
money, wealth, dreams and love.

MANILA

We're not at all alike, thank God. Speak for yourself.

CLIENT

There's something I want to confess to you. I want you to know everything about me, and show you how naked and vulnerable I am.

MANILA

I don't want to know. You're boring me to death with the bullshit you talk.

CLIENT

For years I was in love with a boy the same age as me, Steve. We went to school together, played football together, even slept in the same bed. Steve was always my best friend, but that was all there was to it. We used to pick up foreign girls together. We'd cruise the tourists in the square, take them down to the bridge and screw them stupid. I used to watch him while I was making it with my girl, otherwise I couldn't get it up. I'd shout at him: get into her, Steve, sock it to her, give her one for me! Fuck her ass off!

Third interruption and discussion with the audience.

MANILA

Stop it. You're getting too violent.

CLIENT

It's in the script. The lines are violent, so I say them violently.

MANILA

Well the script's too violent then. Those lines turn my stomach every time I hear you say them.

To the women in the audience.

Aren't you frightened by the violence in those lines? Lots of men talk to women like that. Has that ever happened to you?

To a woman in the audience.

What do you think it means when men see sex that way? Have you ever had any experiences like that?

> *When the discussion is over the houselights go down, and the stage lights go up. The client says his last line and Manila continues with the text.*

MANILA

You're a real fascist.

CLIENT

Bullshit. I'm a socialist. I'm in the democratic party. I used to be in the International Socialists, but I'm more moderate now. I'm still antiviolence though. And I'm all for this new morality – living together in peace and harmony and all that. Anyway, Steve had to do his military service, so all that business came to an end. I got myself a girlfriend, and got serious with her. Now I'm going to marry her.

MANILA

But you still come here to see me.

CLIENT

Marriage is one thing, sex is another. You know how long it is since I last made love with her? Five months. I'm scared I won't even be able to make it with her. I can with you though. Do you think I'm sick?

MANILA

I couldn't care less.

CLIENT

Look, I could marry you!

MANILA

So I could be a full-time whore? No thanks.

CLIENT

A man's offering you his freedom and you turn it down just like that!

MANILA

I don't want your freedom. You'd make me pay for it every single hour, day and night.

CLIENT

Why don't you get a job then? You could be a typist, like my girlfriend. Would you like me to help you look for something?

MANILA

So I can be a whore in an office? No thanks!

CLIENT

You could work as a store clerk.

MANILA

A shop whore? No thanks.

CLIENT

Why are you never satisfied? You make it sound like a prostitute's the only job a woman can do.

MANILA

You said it, snake-eyes. The only choice a woman's got is whether she prostitutes herself in public or private – on the street or at home. Right?

The client comes up to her and kisses her on the neck.

He kisses me, the shit. He kisses me so tenderly my arms just flop. Watch it, Manila, this one's trying to pull a fast one on you. He'll take your breath away, and leave you high and dry and get it all for free. He knows I like his eyebrows, his eyes, his skin. If I look at him any longer I'll fall right into him, like the time I fell right into an old woman on the bus and couldn't get out ... I could feel people looking at my wrinkles in disgust, but I was so lightheaded I thought my brain had flown away. My head was like a shrivelled nut full of black dust. I had a big green bag on my lap and every so often my withered fingers checked that the catch was fastened. I was chewing away like an old goat, and my watery eyes were looking out the window at the ugly and remote world outside. Under my arms I could feel my thighs pressing together but not touching. My heart was beating sluggishly and I couldn't care less about anybody else, all I wanted to do was eat a lovely cake I had in my green bag. That was why I kept checking the clasp of the bag, I was scared someone would steal the cake. I knew my life depended on that cake and nothing else mattered. Fucking old woman, I could have strangled her.

CLIENT

You know what I think, Manila? I think you're really quite respectable. I don't believe you're just going to have a wash, get dressed and go back on the street to pick up more clients.

MANILA

I haven't felt a thing for eight months. What the hell's happening to me with this jerk?

To client

You can lay off the flattery, you won't be getting any discount.

CLIENT

What are you talking about? I'm no cheapskate. I'll give you what I owe you, what we agreed on, don't worry. But you haven't got a pimp.

MANILA

I don't need a pimp. I've got a different kind of set-up, with my girlfriends.

CLIENT

What if I told you I'm strong and I do karate, I can beat anybody in a fight, but I like you and I swear to God I won't rip you off, and offered to look after you? I wouldn't cause any trouble, I'd do whatever you say, and all I'd take is a small percentage. Maybe ten percent. What would you say?

MANILA

I'd say no.

CLIENT

Goddamn it, Manila, I'll leave that ghost of a girlfriend, I'll leave home, I'll leave the university. We could live together, go on a trip together to Paris, Madrid, South America. What do you say?

MANILA

To audience.

What a sense of order there is inside this shitty mint-eyed bastard. Everything clean and tidy, all the furniture neatly arranged, soft carpet under your feet. His family sit on straight, hard-backed chairs: his mother with her mouth full of fish, his fiancee with see-though glass arms, his father with a lead ass. In the middle there's a big comfortable armchair just for him, the favorite son. He's got a big bowl of golden coins on his lap, fresh from the mint. Everything is so neat and tidy inside. Everyone's smiling kindly and affectionately. Then they show me there's a place for me too, on top of a kind of altar. His father takes me up there and forces me to go down on all fours. Then he ties me up with cold, heavy gold cords, still smiling sweetly. Now I'm tied up tight to the wall and the floor. After a while two hands grab my bare breasts, squeeze them and pull them down towards the floor with a savage jerk. Under my belly there's a bucket the milk spurts into with a metallic noise. The pain takes my breath away.

CLIENT

Hey, Manila! What are you doing? Were you asleep? What sort of prostitute are you? You spend all your time day-dreaming, off in a world of your own!

MANILA

I wish I didn't need your body. Or any man's body.

CLIENT

You need me just like I need you. We should join forces, Manila, and make a deal. Its our destiny.

MANILA

No. Just pay up. I don't want to make any deals with you.

CLIENT

Don't you like me?

MANILA

Yes, I do like you. That's just the point. It's a trap. So pay up and get out.

CLIENT

If I pay you I'm finished with you, don't you realize? I want to start something. This could be the start of something new ...

MANILA

Look, I've had enough. Give me my money!

CLIENT

How are you going to make me pay, darling? What'll you do if I refuse to pay? Call the cops? Pull a gun? Look at you – you're small, you've got no muscles, you're exhausted, you haven't even got a dick. What could you do about it? I'm going to go right out that door and leave you. *Ciao!* Just to show you you need a pimp. No one would dare treat you like this if I was looking after you. See?

MANILA

Don't be an asshole. Pay me what you owe me. Weren't you talking about the new morality before? Well you can start by keeping your end of the bargain.

CLIENT

Getting rid of prostitution is part of the new morality. A new society of peace and harmony! There, I'll give you half. You can have the rest next time. *Ciao, amore!*

Manila goes to the door and hollers.

MANILA

Anna! Carmela! Marina! He won't pay up!
Quick, he's going!

*Shouts and blows are heard, and sounds of
protest. Then, a baby crying. Manila goes
and gets her baby and carries it in. She sits
and sings to it.*

Ninna nanna child of mine
Sleep tight don't worry about your future
I'll sew your lips together with string
So you won't be tempted to kiss anyone
You'll say your mother was a witch
You'll say your mother was a fairy godmother
I'll sew up your cunt with silken thread
So you won't be tempted to fuck anyone
You'll say your mother was a witch
You'll say your mother was a fairy godmother
Sleep my baby, eat and get fat
I'll sew up your eyes with verdigris
So you won't be tempted to look at anyone
You'll say your mother was a witch
You'll say your mother was a fairy godmother
When you grow up you'll live with other women
And you'll be a witch, a fairy godmother.

END

Dreams
of Clytemnestra

Translated by Tim Vode

Preface

Real events, dreams, and fantasies are commingled in this play, the setting of which has been moved from ancient Greece to modern Italy. In the play, Maraini turns to a pre-Christian myth of a female goddess, a subterranean divinity, an ancient Mediterranean earth mother who nurtured diverse people and diverse beliefs. 'The myth of Clytemnestra contains the folk belief of a dark-hued madonna, seductive, nurturant, strong, and angry,' writes Lucia Chavola Birnbaum, in commenting on Maraini's play.*

The dreamlike quality of the play creates a surrealist overtone. Here, Orestes does not actually kill his mother, Clytemnestra, as he does in Aeschylus' 'Oresteia,' but he fantasizes doing it. Here, Clytemnestra does not kill Agamemnon; he dies of a heart attack. But both Agamemnon and Clytemnestra imagine her killing him. Our dreams are more real than, or as real as, reality?

Trapped in a patriarchal society, this modern-day Clytemnestra is a lusty, passionate, practical

---

* *Op. cit.*

179

wife and mother. She is full of conflicting emotions – a complex character. We see what happens when a woman stands up in the world of a male power structure. Maraini looks at the contemporary Italian political and cultural climate, whose roots lie in the gender chauvinism of the ancient Greek world, where theatre itself was born. The figure of Clytemnestra plays out her cultural destiny, as she unnaturally disrupts the male order.

Despite Agamemnon's brutal treatment of women (he murders his daughter Iphigenia and rapes Cassandra, his sexual war prize) the chorus in Aeschylus' trilogy mourns his death as that of one who fought a war for a woman (Helen) and then is killed by a woman (Clytemnestra, his wife). In this cultural translation by Maraini, Clytemnestra asks: 'Is that a dream of life or a life of dreaming?' The women chant:

'We are subjugated ... worn out ...
Faithful servants of the father ...
Without a sign from God ...
We do not exist.'

In Maraini's play, Agamemnon has been away in America for ten years. Cassandra is the younger woman whom he meets there. He takes her back with him to Italy. Clytemnestra is the product of a sordid past, including prostitution, incest, and abortions. Agamemnon dreams of his death, but dies of a heart attack. While dying, he imagines Clytemnestra killing him. Clytemnestra, too, dreams it, while Orestes fantasizes about killing her. Clytemnestra is sent to a mental institution; Orestes is exonerated.

The gender chauvinism of the ancient Greeks is made clear. Meanwhile, the surrealism of Maraini's style probes our awarness of the vividness of our dreams, which can seem more real than our everyday lives.

Dreams of Clytemnestra was first performed in English in 1989, by The City Troupe, an off-Broadway theatre company in New York City. The translation was by Tim Vode, co-founder of The City Troupe, and the performance was directed by Greg Johnson, with original music by Michael Sottile. An abstract, dramatic, Dali-esque set was designed for the performance by Marlon Kolsky.

The cast included: *Clytemnestra,* Carmen de Lavallade; *Agamemnon,* Steve Singer; *Electra,* Maggie Rush; *Orestes,* Marko Maglich; *Cassandra,* Wendy Way; *Ægisthus,* Christopher Scotellaro; *Pilot,* Taylor Howard.

Dreams of Clytemnestra

Characters

Clytemnestra
former garment factory worker, now in her own workshop at home.

Agamemnon
Sicilian who has immigrated north to Prato (near Florence)

Electra
apprentice garment worker

Cassandra
American girl

Orestes
Italian immigrant in Germany

Ægisthus
unemployed

Moira
Fury, apparition of the mother, prostitute

Pilot
unemployed student

First Woman, Second Woman, Third Woman
prostitutes, Furies

First, Second, Third Nurse
immigrants to northern Italy

Psychoanalyst
Athena daughter of Zeus, man of science

ACT ONE

CLYTEMNESTRA

Sleeping. What do I need of you! Sleeping!
Just as you abandon me for dead
I hear myself called murderer ... in shadow
I live in shame: you know the guilt that
haunts me, I who from childhood have
suffered what I have suffered, and no god
remembers me, slaughtered by a matricidal hand.
Look, with your heart, at my wounds –
for man sees in sleep only, by day
his eyes look without light.
How you lapped at the things I fed you –
more than wines, like gentle peace-giving
drinks, and evening dishes, cooked in sacred
fires – just as the other gods forgot.
And now see how you trample my gifts –
as he flies, flies like a wild stag, freeing
himself from your hold, so lightly,
it would seem he mocks you ...
Listen to me: I'm telling you my life;
come to your senses, gods of the world
buried under, from deep in your dreams
Clytemnestra calls you!

Iphigenia, standing in a slip, is being dressed as a bride before the audience as if the hall were on a big mirror. She's being dressed with rituals and burial gestures as if for an important ceremony. On another part of the stage, Electra is helping Agamemnon out of his hunting clothes.

AGAMEMNON

They're making me eat shit those sons of bitches.

ELECTRA

You got nothing.

AGAMEMNON

I shot at nothing. A bunch of twigs.

ELECTRA

It's too cold.

AGAMEMNON

Five million they give me. Five million to choke on. And then they get my prize daughter.

ELECTRA

Why don't you eat? You're like an animal.

AGAMEMNON

This animal has stuck his face in it.

ELECTRA

So why don't you sell the shop?

AGAMEMNON

Less than nothing that shop is worth. It's a broken-down wreck. You know what the dog star says? Leave or die.

ELECTRA

They say the ocean's too rough. It scares me it's so angry. It's not stopped howling for a month.

AGAMEMNON

So let it. I have got to go. Your mother is driving me crazy.

ELECTRA

You've got her howling too.

AGAMENNON

Don't talk to me. She sits there shut up in that kitchen and whatever I say is an insult!

ELECTRA

Your marriage means nothing to her.

AGAMENNON

I know. She's a thick-headed, stupid hick; Iphigenia, with how I fixed her couldn't do better.

ELECTRA

She says she's too young to get married.

AGAMEMNON

Wasn't my mother married at thirteen? She had eight kids and held out till ninety. Iphigenia's fourteen, and even worse, she's pregnant.

ELECTRA

They say at the hospital she can't have babies. She could die from it.

AGAMEMNON

They're all con artists and jerks at the hospital. They told my uncle Peppino he had three months to live. That was fifteen years ago and he's healthier than me.

ELECTRA

She didn't even want to see her wedding gown. It looks like an ocean of snow, have you seen it? The dressmaker worked three months on it.

AGAMEMNON

She says her daughter is hers – her breathing, her mouth, her breasts – all hers. And me? What am I? The family garbage? Whose goddamn sperm filled her belly? Whose thoughts created that white skin, who wanted, made, dreamed her? She's not hers, she's mine.

ELECTRA

From father to grandfather, it's men that make
us.

AGAMEMNON

Electra, learn this: From here, from this head
comes everything you need. In my thoughts you
were born. Your mother put her guts to it. I put
the truth. Understand? And now I'm telling
you. Before I go I want everything worked out.
Iphigenia gets a husband for a loan. You and
your mother at the shop with enough to eat.
Orestes in Germany with good work. It's the
only way the family will stay together till I come
back.

ELECTRA

When do you come back?

AGAMEMNON

When I've stuffed my pockets. Without money
I won't. I'm fed up, breaking my neck at that
factory, living in hock. I'm fed up, taking crap
from those Shylocks who run this town.

> *Iphigenia comes in tied to a bed. This is a
> sacrifice. Band music is heard. Agamemnon
> makes a toast to her.*

AGAMEMNON

Here before us, the ocean has turned its angry
face, now meek and gentle as a new bride. And
now, as I prepare to leave, I give away my
daughter, with all the honor and respect of her
entire family. Yes, her mother is still bitter, and
yet with patience and love I will bring her around.
So, allow me to propose a toast from a poor
father off to fight against the rich! Farewell!
Here's to the newlyweds!

> *He throws a kiss to the newlyweds and*
> *leaves. Blackout.*
> *A woman's scream is heard. On a black*
> *backdrop a spray of fireworks. It is the wed-*
> *ding party.*

MOIRA

Blessed gods
Her father motioned to the servants
and, like a lamb bound for slaughter
and brutally tied down,
she was taken, gagged, and strung up.

WOMAN

He killed his daughter with his own hands.
So his ship could leave.

MOIRA

Oh, how brightly burned her eyes
with sadness before the executioner!
And she seemed like a vision, a silent vision,
she who so often had sung
for her father
at royal banquets!

> *Clytemnestra and Electra working at the garment shop.*

CLYTEMNESTRA

What terrible dreams I had last night!

ELECTRA

It must have been lice.

CLYTEMNESTRA

Your father tried to cut my throat with a knife.

ELECTRA

You cut it yourself. You own throat, your own
hands, your own knife, your own dreams.

CLYTEMNESTRA

It was that knife he's always got in his pocket,
the one with the ivory handle, the one with
Diana's head carved on it.

ELECTRA

I was the one who gave him that knife.

CLYTEMNESTRA

He had some strange woman with him, half human and half bird. He said, 'This is my new wife.' Then he started laughing and I saw he'd lost all his teeth.

ELECTRA

Better he told you about it in a dream.

CLYTEMNESTRA

What?

ELECTRA

The woman is real. She's prettier than you, and younger. She's an American girl with long hair down to her knees. Her voice is like honey. He's bringing her here and will make you choke.

CLYTEMNESTRA

What do you know about it, bitch?

ELECTRA

He wrote me. It seems she's some sort of medusa and can see the future. She has eyes like an owl and can see at night as well as day. She's not a gypsy, though. The only things she eats are roses and raw meat, and she pisses perfume. She dances like a snake and under her dress she keeps cool evergreen that soothes and calms him the minute he rests his head.

CLYTEMNESTRA

He told you that?

ELECTRA

I always know what he's doing. I know it with my guts before I ever see it. His letters arrive and I know everything they say. He's got a few gray hairs, your husband. He's depressed and sick to tears for being away so long. Every night he dreams of this empty house. And I wait up for him with open arms. While you, with your belly stuffed with shit, sleep.

CLYTEMNESTRA

You're always spying on me, even when I sleep. I can feel your eyes glued to me and my dreams are black and sticky.

ELECTRA

The little bunny's wandered off and screwed the whole world and now she's fast asleep with heavy dreams of strange sperm.

CLYTEMNESTRA

Everything I do is poison. Everything he does goes down like honey.

ELECTRA

He's my father and your husband.

CLYTEMNESTRA

Ever since Iphigenia died with that baby I stopped thinking of him as my husband.

ELECTRA

He'll come back. He'll put everything like it should be in this broken-down house. He'll buy new machines for the shop, hire new workers, and give us a rest. We'll all celebrate and he'll fix you, little wifey, right back in your place.

CLYTEMNESTRA

That's none of you business.

ELECTRA

I know everything about you, when you leave, when you come back, who you see, where you go, how you spend the money he sends you, when you put on that sticky perfume you smear around the house like some slime, when you get up in your red dress and high heels – I know what's in your heart, you insulting mother of mine.

CLYTEMNESTRA

I don't have to answer to you for what I do.

ELECTRA

Don't hide it, you hate him and would kill him if you could.

CLYTEMNESTRA

He had my daughter butchered. I don't forget.
He sold her to a creditor for five million –
money he needed to pay his debts and leave. He
condemned her to death with that baby; knowing
she'd die, he sacrificed her anyway so he could
go.

ELECTRA

You know perfectly well he couldn't stay. Things
made him. His debts were eating him alive. All
the factories were closed and everyone fired. He
was faced with the same choice, like everyone
else: Buy your looms from us at cost, set up your
shops at home, and we'll buy back the lousy rags
you turn out! And take your old looms and junk
them! He was robbed blind. But then everyone
had to swallow it. After all, was there a choice.
And so, clobbered with debts everyone set up
shop at home. Every house with its own one,
two, five looms; grandmothers, children, relatives
put to work; no timeclock, rest or breaks; day
and night, night and day. There was no stopping
for anyone; he simply did what everyone else
did: put his family to work. And you more than
anyone know how we broke our backs, you, me,
Orestes, even Iphigenia with her bad heart who
could barely stand the vibrating.

CLYTEMNESTRA

But he had big ideas. He kept wanting more machines, more work, more profits.

ELECTRA

Which is why he made so many debts and couldn't pay them.

CLYTEMNESTRA

So what did the others do? How come the others stayed and he left?

ELECTRA

The others come from here; they had relatives who helped them with work in some pig farm or orchard in the country. Not us. We were outsiders from a strange place. And you know how lousy it was in this neighborhood, packed in with everyone like us, mocked for how we think, how we speak and no one to understand.

CLYTEMNESTRA

But things have changed now, Electra. We are here now, drinking the same water, speaking the same language.

ELECTRA

Nothing has changed. Us for us and them for them. You don't understand a thing. Look how we live, always apart, pent up in this neighborhood with nothing but Sicilians like you, or Calabrese or Napolitans.

CLYTEMNESTRA

What does that have to do with anything. He sold his daughter and left.

ELECTRA

He had to. Even you saw how he wept when he married her.

CLYTEMNESTRA

Fourteen, pregnant and sick.

ELECTRA

Envy is eating you up. You don't like it that he's coming home rich with another wife younger and prettier than you. It really gets you, him taking the house back. You're getting old, mother; take a look at the lines in your face, at your hands; look at yourself, at how you're falling apart. How could a man who's still strong and handsome keep you in bed?

CLYTEMNESTRA

You, Electra, like me get up at five, and like me clean the house bent in two with your back aching. It's still dark even when we get to coffee, with our mouths dry, our eyes closed, broken sleep still in our throats. Then like me you sit down to the loom. You set up the pins like I do, you turn the switch and the motor starts, and there we are bombarded by that incredible noise torturing us all day. You sit in front of me, just past the spindles spinning like crazy, and I see you but you don't see me. The spools race up and down pounding like thunder and shaking the house for hours. You and me face to face. I am your equal. Another woman who smells like onions and laundry. A woman like you. But you never look at me, you never see me, always thinking of him on the other side of the ocean, with some black cloud over your head. You, my daughter, a woman, like me – instead of siding with me you live for him, you lick the ground he walks on, you keep his bed warm, you spy for him, you stand watch like his dog.

ELECTRA

He's my father.

CLYTEMNESTRA

And I'm your mother.

ELECTRA

You spit on our family. You think only of your-self. You've never loved this house. For you it's always his – the thief, the criminal who sold your daughter. You live to get even for the dead and you forget about the living. Here Orestes is in Germany and you're not even interested in knowing how he's doing. He sends you money and you can't even thank him. And for me, it's all the same to you if I live or die. All you think about is that sexy body of yours. about decking it out, pampering it, making it fancier. And then free as a bird you go out with that pompous moron Ægisthus who comes over to chow down in your husband's chair like he was dead.

CLYTEMNESTRA

I never took vows to be a nun.

ELECTRA

You'd be happy if he dropped dead, say it!

CLYTEMNESTRA

Left alone for ten years and now he comes and wants back his house, his shop, his wife and his children.

ELECTRA

You were a beggar in the street when he found you. Don't you think everybody in the neighborhood knows it? You think I could forget it?

CLYTEMNESTRA

You and him are cut from the same mold, the same brain. You've banded together to get me.

Moira alone

MOIRA

Perhaps, this very moment, there's someone alive talking about us if we were dead, we who instead believe him dead ...

Agamemnon and Cassandra in a hotel room.

AGAMEMNON

Wake up, Cassandra, it's late. They're waiting for us downstairs for dinner.

CASSANDRA

I dreamed someone was butchering you. With that knife you always carry. They were cutting your throat ...

AGAMEMNON

Where's that bag with the money and credit cards?

CASSANDRA

God, how I was crying! I couldn't do anything for you and you bled to death.

AGAMEMNON

Goddamit, where is that bag? We're screwed if we lost that bag. You too.

CASSANDRA

Dead children were playing in front of your house. Why don't we stay here at the hotel? That house of yours in Prato scares me.

AGAMEMNON

Your eyes are swollen like two golf balls. Get up and help me find that fucking bag.

CASSANDRA

That house of yours has a sick, sweet smell, I know it, like something somewhere is rotting under the floor. Let's stay here Agamemnon, or you go without me.

AGAMEMNON

You're my woman and you come with me.

CASSANDRA

I'm not your wife and I'm not about to forget it.

AGAMEMNON

You live with me, you sleep with me, you take my mouth and lay on me; you're always around, always here, and you're not my woman?

CASSANDRA

Why didn't we stay back home?

AGAMEMNON

Here it is! I hid it so well I almost didn't find it.
Now get on your shoes and let's go.

CASSANDRA

Why don't you go meet your wife ahead of me?
I don't know what to say. I'm afraid.

AGAMEMNON

Look, you're my secretary, my bookkeeper, my
administrator, my associate, what does it matter.
You're with me and they'll have to accept you.

CASSANDRA

Why did you bring me here? I didn't want to
come. That house will devour me, I know it.
Your wife's got her back up and is ready to
pounce.

AGAMEMNON

Don't talk nonsense. Clytemnestra is a good
wife. She respects what it means to be a family,
she lives in a neighborhood with people like us,
and she's used to doing what she's told and
working hard.

CASSANDRA

God, with the blood spurting from your neck! I tried to stop it with my blouse, with my skirt, and I was drenched with it, but still you died and there was nothing I could do.

AGAMEMNON

I don't want to hear it. It's bad luck. Now get dressed and let's go.

CASSANDRA

I wish I were still on that boat.

AGAMEMNON

Shut up in some cabin, choking from the heat. No, not for me.

CASSANDRA

But it was so beautiful at night, on the deck with everyone there and the music. There was that boy who played the guitar, you remember, the one from third class who always came up to first. He wanted me, that boy, and he would have had me.

AGAMEMNON

Sure he wanted you but you're not to be had. You're not free.

CASSANDRA

That's what I told him. He had eyes like some starving animal.

AGAMEMNON

It was amazing. You falling all over him. You were ridiculous.

CASSANDRA

I took this trip for you. Because I love you.

AGAMEMNON

I told you, I don't care about love. All I care about is loyalty. I don't need love. I don't give a shit about love.

CASSANDRA

Loyalty without loving ends up in fear.

AGAMEMNON

You're right: fear. It's good you're scared. Everyone's scared. Everyone's always scared. You think it's love that made me leave my wife and children, living in hock in some foreign place. You think it's love that made me swallow my pride to get what I got taking insults and abuse from those animals you call Americans. You think it's love that made me come back for my house and my workshop after ten years in exile?

CASSANDRA

God, how the blood was spurting!

AGAMEMNON

It's fear that made me go, fear that made me work and fear that brought me back. And it's fear that'll make me a whole new shop and fear that'll make me rich.

CASSANDRA

You think you'll find everything the same after ten years, but you're dreaming. Your wife will be someone else. You won't recognize her. Your house will be different. You'll hate it.

AGAMEMNON

My wife is nothing more, nothing less than what I made her. When I married her in Sicily she was fourteen years old. She had no father, no mother, and was dragging herself around the streets selling herself for a piece of bread. I took her and made her what I wanted. She can't change because she's what I made. She's just like me. She wants me. She belongs to me.

CASSANDRA

And what about me? Where do I fit in?

AGAMEMNON

You're my strength, my success. With you I
shared my bed and took on America. With you
I made money. I can't leave you.

CASSANDRA

Your wife will want you all for herself.

AGAMEMNON

My wife will stay in her place, like she's supposed
to. She won't want anything more than I give
her. She'll swallow her jealousy and pay you
respect. And if she wants a divorce, she's a free
woman. But she won't get a dime from me. Let
her try!

CASSANDRA

Oh Lord of wanderers, you've lost me.
This is the second time you've lost me.
Where are you taking me? To what kind of
house?

Agamemnon alone

AGAMEMNON

Now let me enter my house,
let me give thanks to the gods who've carried me
so far, who've led me here
with Victory at my side, my companion.
Few are the men ready to pay homage,
without envy, to a friend who's found fortune.

When bitterness infects a heart,
a double pain it brings the afflicted:
To suffer the weight of his own hurt,
and to see before him another's happiness.

Ægisthus and Clytemnestra

ÆGISTHUS

Did you go to bed with him?

CLYTEMNESTRA

He came home with someone else. Yes, I went to
bed with him.

ÆGISTHUS

You said you wouldn't go to bed with any man.

CLYTEMNESTRA

But it wasn't just any bed. It was my bed. He's
my husband.

ÆGISTHUS

You should leave him. Come with me.

CLYTEMNESTRA

And how would we live?

ÆGISTHUS

I'd work.

CLYTEMNESTRA

You've been saying that for years. Without me you couldn't survive. And I've got the workshop.

ÆGISTHUS

Move it away.

CLYTEMNESTRA

I can't. It's his by law. He bought it. But who worked there for ten years? Who put her life and guts in it?

ÆGISTHUS

So what do we do?

CLYTEMNESTRA

Nothing. We wait. Maybe he'll end up going back to America. By now he's not used to this city. He's got big ideas, he wants to start a whole factory, but everything will slip through his fingers before he knows it.

ÆGISTHUS

You shouldn't go to bed with him again.

CLYTEMNESTRA

He's the one who comes in my bed.

ÆGISTHUS

Tell him about me.

CLYTEMNESTRA

So he can have an excuse to divorce me and not give up a dime.

ÆGISTHUS

I'll get work.

CLYTEMNESTRA

You can't, Ægisthus. How long did the last job I found you last? Not even ten days.

ÆGISTHUS

It was a disgusting job.

CLYTEMNESTRA

All jobs are disgusting.

ÆGISTHUS

Five hundred thousand lire a month.

CLYTEMNESTRA

You don't start at much.

ÆGISTHUS

But I'm twenty-eight. I can't work at some kid's job.

CLYTEMNESTRA

Why not? Till now you've let your mother take care of you, dragging the university around like it was some dead tail stuck to your rear.

ÆGISTHUS

What a big deal, like some sheik, your husband
makes of himself for that big two cents he scraped
up over there. Who knows what he thinks.

CLYTEMNESTRA

He thinks what he is: a sharp, cunning man who
knows how to get money from rape. And now
that he's rich he's waiting for everyone to start
depending on him, thanking him, and making a
big deal over him. It's normal.

ÆGISTHUS

I could kill him.

CLYTEMNESTRA

I already did. After Iphigenia died.

ÆGISTHUS

But there he is alive and wanting you in his bed.

CLYTEMNESTRA

I'm making love to a corpse.

ÆGISTHUS

He disgusts you, tell me he disgusts you!

He doesn't disgust me. He's a gentle, passionate corpse. He smells like dried carobs. I remember in Sicily when we first met. He lived with a beautiful woman whose head was wrapped in bandages. I was a wild woman, screwing whatever came along. I'd run away from the reformatory and I was sleeping in parks. I ate what I stole from stores. He gave me a bed and hot food and we made love, the three of us, the woman with the bandages, him, and me. Our sheets had that smell of dried carobs. Every morning she vomited. Every evening she vomited. I don't know what she had. I used to hold her forehead. At night she'd hold me close to her. He was jealous. He's scream. I'd laugh, I didn't give a damn about anything. For me it was enough to eat and sleep. But then one day he got tired of living that way, the three of us, and he wanted to toss me back out in the street. He said, 'I'll find you a husband, I'll give you money'. But I didn't want a husband or any money. I wanted him. I was in love with him. The woman in bandages begged him to keep me. And I stayed. But she died. And we came to Prato. I had two children before he married me. He was jealous. He wanted me for himself, but every time I complained he said: I saved your life, remember it. But he didn't save me, he ate me up.

ÆGISTHUS

You're still in love with him.

CLYTEMNESTRA

I was in love with him when I was fourteen. If he looked at another woman, I died. If he turned his back on me I disappeared. I'd always follow his eyes. I was afraid he'd stop feeling for me. If he stopped feeling for me I died. My life depended on what he felt. When he stopped loving me I'd stop breathing. I wanted to feel his foot on top of me to know I was still living, somewhere in my sleeping body. That's how it was for years and years: Him stepping on me, walking all over me, and me hoping only not to bother him too much, not to get kicked out. I had so many abortions. With the second baby he married me, whether for kindness, gratitude, comfort, I don't know. I kept on thanking him. Only when he decided to give away my daughter to pay his debts was the spell of loving him broken. I stopped loving him. I didn't hate him even. I wanted him to end up with his throat slit in some ditch so as not to see him. You saw how happy she was at the wedding, her with her tiny pregnant stomach. She loved her gown and the whole big party. Her husband took her like you take on a responsibility. She had a beautiful home with beautiful furniture and she immediately gave in to playing the housewife.

With that dead husband, with no love, she had two cars she couldn't drive, and she was happy, satisfied. Then she died for the baby nobody wanted; she knew she'd died, they'd warned her at the hospital, and still she tried to make it through and she didn't.

ÆGISTHUS

He sold his daughter. He keeps you tied up because that's how he likes it. He's always wanted two women. He's using you. Turn him in.

CLYTEMNESTRA

For what? For having a wife who works, a secretary who helps him, a daughter who workships him, and a community that welcomes him with open arms?

ÆGISTHUS

He sold his daughter.

CLYTEMNESTRA

But she went along with it. And then where is it written that he got money from the family. All he did was take his beautiful and pregnant daughter to the altar. How many other fathers would have done the same? It was just a way of making things right, of giving her some security, some money, a house.

ÆGISTHUS

You are not to go back to that bed.

CLYTEMNESTRA

I do what I want, how I want.

Three beds: Cassandra, Agamemnon, and Clytemnestra

CASSANDRA

Are you asleep?

CLYTEMNESTRA

No.

CASSANDRA

He is. He looks satisfied. He's glad he made us both happy. He's been waiting for this day like it was Easter morning. His faithful wife from home on one side and his woman from abroad on the other.

CLYTEMNESTRA

And are you happy?

CASSANDRA

I could kill you.

CLYTEMNESTRA

You, I could stick a knife in your throat. You've seen that knife he always keeps in his pocket, the one he changes the looms with, fixes the settings and cuts the strings. It cuts sharper that a razor and goes straight to the heart.

CASSANDRA

And you wouldn't kill him?

CLYTEMNESTRA

Before you.

CASSANDRA

He thinks you're still in love with him.

CLYTEMNESTRA

Like oil and vinegar.

CASSANDRA

But I saw you under him. You love him.

CLYTEMNESTRA

I gave him his rights as a husband, nothing more.

CASSANDRA

I could have torn you apart.

CLYTEMNESTRA

I don't feel a thing, not a thing.

CASSANDRA

You have someone else?

CLYTEMNESTRA

First we saw each other out of the neighborhood, in the parks, outside the armory. But then it got cold and we didn't know where to make love. So I told him to come home with me. He'd whistle to me from the street and I'd open a window for him. Everyone knew it in the neighborhood but they made like they didn't. For the people here, a woman who betrays her husband loses respect. They all think like in the old country, especially women. And they're always judging, judging, even if they did know my husband was gone so long, and that he'd left, dumping me alone. But they didn't stop talking to me. It was enough that I didn't bring it into the open. At night I was free. Now I'm not, now I can't do anything. Now I'm here with him, you, and my dreams to choke me.

CASSANDRA

You've taken an incredible load off my mind. Here I thought I was going to die of jealousy and you've let me breathe again. I want to do something for you. What can I do?

CLYTEMNESTRA

Take him away from here. There's not enough for him to sink his teeth into here. He's already a foreigner, he's made his money and he has what he needs. Let him leave his two broken-down old looms for us. Take him away, back to your country.

CASSANDRA

Your husband's a stubborn man. He wants to set up a new workshop, buy new looms, new machines, and put lots of people to work for him.

CLYTEMNESTRA

I'd love to slit his throat, Cassandra. But now I'm going to sleep. Give me your hand. It's late.

The two women go to sleep hand in hand.

CASSANDRA

Don't look at me like some bird crying
frightened in the trees: all I want is
when I'm dead you bear me witness
to the day when for my woman's blood
another woman's blood will flow, and when
for a man's blood, killed by his wife,
another man's blood will flow. This is the favor
I ask of my hosts before I die.

Orestes and Pilot.

ORESTES

They've got Salvo. They locked him up.

PILOT

Your old Prato is a sad place! Cold in the winter, boiling in the summer, always buzzing with nasty flies in the air, and everyone working shut up in their houses, mean and sober, working, working, even on Sunday, even at night. Your home town is certainly not an amusing place, everyone's so responsible. No one has any fun. They're all dreaming. Black and nervous dreams, raving dreams. Think of all the slimey dreams mixing around in the rag bins back home!

ORESTES

He already worked at the shop when he was seven. His father used to tie him down so he wouldn't escape. Once when he cut the rope, his father beat him with a belt.

PILOT

He was part of a gang of thieves.

ORESTES

He came from people like mine. He had a motorcycle.

PILOT

You could have been one of them too.

ORESTES

If I hadn't gone to Germany, maybe.

PILOT

Like Gino, the mousy one. He's one friend of yours I don't like.

ORESTES

A million times we played marbles under his steps. His mother would fix him lunch with eggs and home-made bread. He always gave me some if I traded tobacco. We used to piss together against the same tree.

PILOT

I don't like how he looks with that vacant stare.

ORESTES

For a few months I worked for his uncle who owns a bakery. We'd deliver bread on bicycles. Now he's got an Alfa Romeo. He makes money off of women. He began with his sister, then his fiancee. When he was a kid, he used to stutter and wear pants with patches and he was afraid of everything. Now he's completely different: he smokes like a demon, wears rings all over his fingers, and he talks and jokes like some big shot. He lost all his teeth in a motorcycle accident. He wears dentures. But all the women like him. He's free with money. He's always giving everyone presents. Part of the money he makes he gives to his mother. They live like a hundred years ago in his house, with his father barking orders, his mother never speaking and slaving like the maid, and his sister who has to be home by eight. And with all that she's a prostitute and he's her pimp.

PILOT

And none of them are like you?

ORESTES

All of them. We're all the same even though we do different things.

PILOT

Yeah, like your other friend, Gaetano.

ORESTES

Deadfish? No, Deadfish has another story: he joined the communist party. He organizes committees. He's chapter secretary for his district. He got married at nineteen and his wife's having a baby. He's very together. He'll end up with a career.

PILOT

And none of them were forced abroad for the same reasons as you?

ORESTES

Atreo, the saddest one. He left because of debts too. But then he was gone for six months and went back. His mother died when he was a year old. His father's a janitor. He went to school. He wears a chain with a big black 'A' around his neck. He says he's an anarchist. He beats his father because he doesn't give him money, and because he drinks. He's a piece of cake with his friends. With his family, he's a madman. And still his father supports him. But he keeps saying he's a shit.

PILOT

And the others?

ORESTES

The others are all the same. You see them hanging around the bar with their skin-tight pants. They all either live off some woman, or by stealing, or getting into trouble. But at home they all conform. They all live this double life. Good boys who love their mothers at home, never talking a word back, nothing. Outside they cut loose. But they all mean well, inside or out. They're not phonies. They're just divided – like me, like everyone.

MOIRA

Children, future of the family line,
Silence! Let no one hear you, children!
In the days when God brings wine
if a sudden breeze blows through the house,
it is because the master returns, to his abode
to live out the destiny which is his.

Agamemnon and Cassandra.

AGAMEMNON

Help, help, they're killing me!

CASSANDRA

You're just sleeping, my love.

AGAMEMNON

Shouting.

I'm dying Cassandra, help me!

CASSANDRA

It's just a bad dream.

AGAMEMNON

They've slit my throat.

CASSANDRA

You're just sleeping, don't worry.

AGAMEMNON

Look, I'm covered with blood, look, I'm dying.

CASSANDRA

You're all sweaty, you've got a fever.

AGAMEMNON

That knife I always keep in my pocket, the one with the ivory handle.

CASSANDRA

Who's killing you?

AGAMEMNON

My wife. I recognized her hand. She'd covered her face, but it was her, I know it.

CASSANDRA

It's only a bad dream.

AGAMEMNON

She kept digging till she found the vein and then she pulled back. I couldn't move my arms. I kept screaming but nothing came out. She was sitting with her knees on my chest, and she kept pushing, pushing that knife in me.

CASSANDRA

You're just sleeping, don't worry.

AGAMEMNON

She struck me dead.

CASSANDRA

You're burning up, you have a fever.

AGAMEMNON

Look at all the blood I'm losing, I'm soaked.

CASSANDRA

Go to sleep, my love.

AGAMEMNON

The knife with the ivory handle, the one with that terrible face of Diana the avenger carved on it.

CASSANDRA

That wife of yours talks gentle but her eyes are cold and bitter.

AGAMEMNON

I kept screaming but nothing came out. I couldn't move my arms. My eyes stayed open but I couldn't see.

CASSANDRA

That's how your daughter Iphigenia died.

AGAMEMNON

It was my wife. I recognized her hand. She'd covered her face, but it was her, I know it.

CASSANDRA

Go to sleep my love.

AGAMEMNON

She plunged the knife in my chest. I'd just come out of the shower, my white bathrobe was drenched with blood.

CASSANDRA

It's just a bad dream.

AGAMEMNON

The knife with Diana's face.

CASSANDRA

You're really sweating, you have a fever.

AGAMEMNON

I kept screaming, but nothing came out. I couldn't move my arms. She was sitting with her knees on my chest, and she kept pushing, pushing that knife in me.

CASSANDRA

Who was it?

AGAMEMNON

My wife. She'd covered her face but I recognized her. It was her.

CASSANDRA

It's just a bad dream, relax.

AGAMEMNON

I'm dying, Cassandra, help me.

CASSANDRA

Go to sleep, my love.

AGAMEMNON

They slit my throat.

CASSANDRA

That's how Iphigenia died in that old dream of yours.

AGAMEMNON

Look, I'm covered with blood, look, I'm dying!

CASSANDRA

One murder dream brings on more murder dreams. Just sleep, it's nothing.

AGAMEMNON

Help me, I'm dying!

CASSANDRA

Go to sleep, hold me. It's just a fearful dream.

Agamemnon dies. Cassandra sings a lullaby.

MOIRA

Oh, my lord, my poor lord
how will I mourn your?
What can my faithful heart say?
There you are, in the spider's web,
left lifeless by a guilty hand.

Clytemnestra and Ægisthus.

CLYTEMNESTRA

I killed my husband.

ÆGISTHUS

You didn't kill him. He died.

CLYTEMNESTRA

I dug a knife in his flesh, so many times my
wrists hurt.

ÆGISTHUS

You didn't kill him, Clytemnestra. He died. He
had a heart attack.

CLYTEMNESTRA

He looked at me with those eagle eyes of his.
How I loved him, Ægisthus, how I will mourn
those eyes!

ÆGISTHUS

You're all sweaty, you have a fever.

CLYTEMNESTRA

I killed my husband, I killed him with my own
hands, Ægisthus.

ÆGISTHUS

Now the house will be ours, the workshop will
be ours. We can set up a whole new business
with the money he left.

CLYTEMNESTRA

He kept on looking at me: Even when he was
dead, he kept on staring at me with those crazy
jealous eyes. I'll never love another like him.

ÆGISTHUS

He was a big man. A man with guts and courage.
He lived through emigration, he made it back.
He died. He had a bad heart.

CLYTEMNESTRA

I killed my husband, Ægisthus, what do I do?

ÆGISTHUS

You're really all sweaty, you have a fever.

CLYTEMNESTRA

That knife with Diana's head on it, you know how many times I stuck it in his chest? And he wouldn't die; he kept writhing, screaming, spurting out blood, but he wouldn't die.

ÆGISTHUS

Now we'll have the workshop for ourselves, the house for ourselves. His bed will be mine.

CLYTEMNESTRA

The first stab I did here, above his ribs. But I didn't touch his heart. I saw his mouth gasp. Then I stabbed higher, at the base of his neck. The blood spurted over my wrists. And he made the exact same movements Iphigenia did when she was butchered. With the same furious precision, the same passionate strength. I felt his blood like he felt his daughter's blood run over his bare arms.

ÆGISTHUS

You'll be my wife.

CLYTEMNESTRA

I tore apart his pride. I can still feel the warmth on my wrists.

ÆGISTHUS

All you are is tired, my love, you're not guilty.

CLYTEMNESTRA

I'll never love another like him, Ægisthus.

ÆGISTHUS

Now we'll live together.

CLYTEMNESTRA

I've tasted revenge. I'm drunk on it. But now, what do I do?

ÆGISTHUS

Now it's just us, you and me. We'll take what's ours.

CLYTEMNESTRA

I killed him to get back my daughter, to get back my workshop.

ÆGISTHUS

He was a big man. A courageous man. He lived through emigration. He made it back. He died of natural causes. He had a weak heart.

CLYTEMNESTRA

Now I can love him freely, like the murky depths of my dreams.

ÆGISTHUS

You love me now, stop thinking about the dead.

CLYTEMNESTRA

I hate you for your stupid vitality, Ægisthus, for being alive.

ÆGISTHUS

Let's think about us now. The workshop is yours, you've worn yourself down to the bone over it.

CLYTEMNESTRA

I love you for your stubborn greed, Ægisthus, for being in love.

ÆGISTHUS

Give me a kiss.

CLYTEMNESTRA

I dug a knife in his flesh, so many times my wrists hurt.

ÆGISTHUS

Give me a kiss, love, you're mine.

The two embrace.

Electra and Moira accompany the dead body of Agamemnon.

ELECTRA

For your beautiful father's arms.

MOIRA

My lord, my poor lord, how will I mourn you?

ELECTRA

For your proud head like a lion slaughtered.

MOIRA

How will I mourn you.

ELECTRA

For your steely tongue that never told the truth.

MOIRA

How will I mourn you.

ELECTRA

For your nervous, gentle heart.

MOIRA

How will I mourn you.

ELECTRA

For your shadowy limbs.

MOIRA

How will I mourn you.

ELECTRA

For your legs that ran trusting against death.

MOIRA

How will I mourn you.

ELECTRA

For your fiery guts and passionate languors.

MOIRA

How will I mourn you.

ELECTRA

For your eyes that joyfully looked at the world you possessed.

MOIRA

How will I mourn you.

ELECTRA

For your unbreakable bull's neck.

MOIRA

How will I mourn you.

ELECTRA

For your hot blood running like a swollen river.

MOIRA

How will I mourn you.

ELECTRA

I loved this man's body more than myself. Greedily and furiously I loved his sex, without ever touching him, ready to die to give him obedience and pleasure. How will I mourn you, father?

Orestes and Pilot.

ORESTES

I found out my mother has a lover.

PILOT

So?

ORESTES

At her age, as crazy as she looks, it's absurd.

PILOT

After ten years in Germany. After working for the revolution. After our love together. After all our talks on freedom, here you are playing the moralist. It's stupid.

ORESTES

She's my mother.

PILOT

You're jealous, like when you were a boy and hid behind her door to peek at her.

ORESTES

Who told you that bullshit?

PILOT

You did. One night when you couldn't sleep, don't you remember? You also told me how you'd hide in her closet to breathe the smell of her dresses and how you'd hear her voice calling you all through the house.

ORESTES

I never said anything so insipid. And on top of it she's marrying him and the two of them will use my father's bed and take his money.

PILOT

Say what's really bothering you: the money. Your respectable father died without making a will. He obviously didn't expect to die. So who inherits it all now?

ORESTES

Cassandra ran off with part of the cash. We'll never know how much.

PILOT

She did well. They would have left her without a cent.

ORESTES

Seeing him get out of that bed, get washed in that bathroom, eat off the same plates ... what kind of family is that?

PILOT

What do you care about your family?

ORESTES

It's almost incest. He's my father's cousin, and eighteen years younger than him.

PILOT

And what about you? Instead of getting married normally, you're doing it with your own sex. Isn't that a scandal? Isn't it that something to shame your family, to make it the laughing stock of your goddamn neighbors?

ORESTES

You're part of the night. By day you're a friend and that's all.

PILOT

And you can accept living a double life, going out at night like some scared mouse?

ORESTES

My double life is a sickness that only affects me. Yes, I live divided. Why should you expect my neighbors to know about love between men? Why should you expect them to know the German ghetto where we had to live, about how important a warm body is, a body that won't scorn you in a world that does. Living abroad's made us all perverts and failures.

PILOT

Don't talk bullshit. What do you mean, perverts, failures?

ORESTES

My life back home and my life in town, my old ways and my new – none of it will ever come together for me and I'll die of it.

PILOT

Good, evil, bad, good – you think like some simple old lady.

ORESTES

Did you see my sister Electra? She parades in mourning like some crow. Like some bird gorged on old crusts, stupidly, old-age and death. But my past is our past, our family, harmony, childhood, love. I can feel her standing over me at night like she were the mother of my dreams breathing hot and holy in my face.

PILOT

Your sister is out of her mind in love with your father. Open your eyes before you give in to her raving for revenge.

ORESTES

Did you see that medallion she wears around her neck? Inside it there's a lock of my father's hair from when he was a baby. My entire family is there in that gold and glass medallion. I never see her face when I'm with her. All I see is that medallion. It dances in front of my eyes. It goes up and down, up and down bouncing along as she walks. That shiny medallion on that black dress makes my heart thump, my breath stop. There I am, hanging between that woman's breasts, with that hair, that gold, that cut glass, that worn-out chain.

PILOT

You've got a real fetish.

ORESTES

Objects are sometimes more tyrannical than people. I stop being free in front of that pendant.

PILOT

Let's go to bed, it's late.

ORESTES

Are you sleepy?

PILOT

I want to hold your body.

ORESTES

Don't tell me. Do it but don't say it. Quiet is the only talk I can deal with now.

PILOT

So come on. Quietly. With all the hypocrisy we can muster. And we won't upset your proletarian consciousness, or disturb the archaic ravings of your sister, or scandalize the mummified minds of your neighbors.

Orestes before the tomb of Agamemnon.

ORESTES

Father, poor father,
what word, what act
do I need
to bring back your soul
from the depths of earth?
Darkness and light are
one: death song
nearly is life song,
for all Atreans
before this house!

Orestes and Electra.

ELECTRA

You know what you have to do, Orestes.

ORESTES

You've been in mourning too long. Think a little about yourself, about your own life.

ELECTRA

You've got no spine.

ORESTES

You go to church every morning.

ELECTRA

Your eyes are empty.

ORESTES

I don't go to church.

ELECTRA

It has nothing to do with church, but the family.

ORESTES

I don't have a steady hand.

ELECTRA

Germany changed you. You're not a man anymore.

ORESTES

My feelings are dead for the family. Whatever my mother does, I don't care, it's her business.

ELECTRA

But your father is your father. And she killed him.

ORESTES

He died.

ELECTRA

And what about the house and the workshop and the money he brought back from America that he suffered years to make? You don't care that she gets it all, that she's marrying someone who'll give orders around here like some big boss?

ORESTES

We have rights on part of the inheritance.

ELECTRA

We have no rights. There's a will. It just surfaced.

ORESTES

What does it say?

ELECTRA

It says everything's hers. Forged, completely forged.

ORESTES

And where did this will come from?

ELECTRA

From the lawyer.

ORESTES

So how do you know it's forged?

ELECTRA

They tricked him. They forced it out of him at the last minute.

ORESTES

But how if you were there the whole time, if you never left him a minute?

ELECTRA

It's not the money, Orestes, it's the house, it's the workshop. Where do I go if they kick me out of this house? Where do I work? I was born here and I'm going to stay, as my own boss. I'm not letting some stranger take my father's place. I won't let him near his bed, I won't let him sit to eat with us, I won't.

ORESTES

He's not a stranger.

ELECTRA

A miserable relative who's brought our family
far worse than any enemy.

ORESTES

His grandfather and our grandfather were
brothers.

ELECTRA

And they butchered one another for an acre of
land.

ORESTES

Father died from an heart attack. She's free to
remarry.

ELECTRA

That's what they say.

ORESTES

Don't go on. You know how he died. You were
there.

ELECTRA

They bought off everyone, even the doctor. The
will's our proof.

ORESTES

He's dead, at rest.

ELECTRA

You're afraid of her too. I knew that Germany
would turn you to mush. When you were a boy
you used to kill cats with one knife-stroke; you
didn't even give them the chance to breathe.

ORESTES

I was coming from a different place.

ELECTRA

You're afraid.

ORESTES

What do you want me to do?

ELECTRA

What's always been done: Early one morning
when she gets out of bed. No one will see it, and
even if they do, they'll keep quiet.

ORESTES

I don't like it.

ELECTRA

You're a coward.

ORESTES

I don't like it.

ELECTRA

Living abroad is disgusting. When does that
friend of yours leave?

ORESTES

Why?

ELECTRA

I don't like him. He looks like he's laughing at
everything. I don't like him. And he plants bad
thoughts in you. When is he leaving?

ORESTES

He thinks differently than us, but he's fine. And
he's a friend. I don't want you treating him
badly.

ELECTRA

He keeps laughing at me.

ORESTES

What's wrong with laughing?

ELECTRA

He thinks he'll wear me down with that know-
it-all laugh of his.

ORESTES

You're always looking for drama. He wants you
to see the light side.

ELECTRA

The light side of father's death?

ORESTES

There's a light side to everything. Even to us sitting here fighting over some sort of revenge that can't be done.

ELECTRA

He came back a champion, with money; he came back happy, invigorated to take back his house and his workshop, and he got death.

ORESTES

Do you know what conscientious objector means?

ELECTRA

I don't care.

ORESTES

It means someone who refuses to fight war, refuses to kill, refuses to die for something he doesn't believe in.

ELECTRA

I don't care.

ORESTES

I'm a conscientious objector against you, against
the family, against the neighborhood. I don't
like hating and being hated, killing and being
killed, I don't like it, I don't believe in it.

Electra at her father's grave.

ELECTRA

Father, I pray you, help your children!
Father whose death was unbefitting a king
give me the rule of your house!
Free your servant
from the hands of Ægisthus!
Remember the vessel in which you died!
Remember the trap they lay you!
Send love to fight at your children's side,
or rather, send hate, to kill who killed you,
if after losing you now would win.
Do not blot from earth your kindred's seed,
if even dead, dead you would not be.
Children a father rescue from the void
like buoys holding a net
bobbing on a whirlpool suspended ...

Clytemnestra and Electra.

CLYTEMNESTRA

I had a terrible dream.

ELECTRA

Your dreams reek.

CLYTEMNESTRA

I gave birth to a snake. But I loved it because it came from me. I swaddled it, I cared for it. I took it to my breast. And it sucked my nipples.

ELECTRA

A guilty dream.

CLYTEMNESTRA

I cradled the snake, I loved it. I kept waiting for it to fall asleep on my milk. But suddenly I realized horrified that together with the milk it was sucking my blood.

ELECTRA

That dream could be more than a dream.

CLYTEMNESTRA

Whenever I wake up I always find you over me, staring at me. You're the one who brings on these terrible dreams. What do you want from me?

ELECTRA

You've not been a good wife.

CLYTEMNESTRA

What do you know of it?

ELECTRA

You've not been a good mother.

CLYTEMNESTRA

Did I deprive you of something?

ELECTRA

Yes, my family. You took on our family with loathing and disgust. You let your husband go off by himself. You let Orestes go. You never waited for them, loved them, prayed for them. You only thought of yourself, of your stomach.

CLYTEMNESTRA

What do you want from me?

ELECTRA

I want you different. Like grandmother, father's mother, was. A quiet woman who smelled like basil, her being dedicated to the family, ready to take on any sacrifice tenderly, with enthusiasm. Instead you come and go as you please. You hand out decisions like you were the boss, taking, giving orders, but only as you want. And us you treat like some strangers, without a thought.

CLYTEMNESTRA

If you're worried about the will, Electra, there's plenty for you too.

ELECTRA

I'm not worried about the will, but about my life. I won't see any man take my father's place.

CLYTEMNESTRA

He drew up the will before he returned from America. It came late because it was mailed from his lawyer there to our lawyer here. Cassandra knew about it. A lot went to her. The house and the workshop to me. You'll get the stocks, and so will Orestes.

ELECTRA

It's not the money, I'm telling you. it's my future.

CLYTEMNESTRA

You'll find a husband with a house and money enough not to work if you don't want. What more do you expect?

ELECTRA

I'll never get married, mama. I'm staying in this house to keep alive the memory of my father whom you never loved, who died murdered by indifference and neglect.

CLYTEMNESTRA

I don't need you.

ELECTRA

Without me his memory would vanish in a few
months. And with him, our whole family, our
strength, our dignity would vanish.

CLYTEMNESTRA

How I hate this job! How I hate this town! How
I hate this family!

ELECTRA

Does the pain our mothers bring us
ever end?
No. It doesn't.
A starving wolf in my soul,
that's what my mother gave me.
Oh mother, mother,
go away, vicious mother,
you who had the courage
to bury a king in exile
with tears from no mourners
and none of your own!

ACT TWO

At the table: Clytemnestra, Ægisthus, Orestes, Electra.

ORESTES

Why such a big dinner, mama?

CLYTEMNESTRA

Ask Electra. She's the one who made it.

ORESTES

Is it a holiday?

ELECTRA

Yes, the holiday of a family reunited. My mother, my brother, me and him ...

Points to an empty place with a plate in front of it.

ÆGISTHUS

Don't I exist?

ELECTRA

He will be eating with us. From now on. He'll have his own plate, his own silverware, his own wine. He'll keep us company.

CLYTEMNESTRA

It's sad, ugly joke. Let the dead lie in peace.
They don't need your theatrics.

ÆGISTHUS

Your mother's right. The dead are happy where
they are. Why do you want to torture them.

ELECTRA

But there he is, don't you see him? He's got an
open wound spurting blood but he's smiling at
his reunited family.

ÆGISTHUS

Enough, Electra!

CLYTEMNESTRA

She's always been like this. When she was little
she'd set up altars to the dead in her room. She
had her pictures of grandfather and then great
grandfather. She'd put out fresh flowers in front
of their portraits like they were saints. She'd
smash her dolls and then cut off their heads and
bury them in the yard so she could mourn them.

ELECTRA

When did you ever care about my games?

CLYTEMNESTRA

Don't you remember, with Iphigenia, in the back yard?

ELECTRA

Iphigenia maybe, she was your daughter. Not me.

CLYTEMNESTRA

Why, whose daughter were you?

ELECTRA

My father's.

ORESTES

Can't we eat in peace?

ÆGISTHUS

Yes, let's eat in peace. The dead with the dead and the living with the living.

ELECTRA

What lovely company!

ÆGISTHUS

You'd rather be with the dead?

ELECTRA

A hundred times over. Buried even.

ÆGISTHUS

What you need, Electra, is to find a good husband
and have some children. It would improve your
outlook.

ELECTRA

I'm not speaking with that phantom, that
woman.

ÆGISTHUS

Woman? Me?

CLYTEMNESTRA

She's already married, to her dead father. Widow
and virgin.

ELECTRA

My cousin wears a ring with a broken body on it.
A bride of Christ. No one finds that funny.

ÆGISTHUS

You want to become a nun?

ELECTRA

I want my family like it was before.

CLYTEMNESTRA

But if your father is dead …

ELECTRA

A family of dead people is sometimes better than a family of living ones.

CLYTEMNESTRA

You're morbid. You've taken away my appetite.

ELECTRA

That's what I wanted.

ORESTES

A mother who's not a mother is not a woman.

ÆGISTHUS

Respect your mother, she's expecting a baby.

CLYTEMNESTRA

Why did you tell him?

ÆGISTHUS

Because I don't like how he treats you, how he speaks to you. Look at her, she's a mother carrying a baby in her womb.

ORESTES

You're having a baby, mama, at your age?

CLYTEMNESTRA

I'm forty-five years old, Orestes, and I'm not dead yet.

ÆGISTHUS

You see, Electra, at forty-five years of age, a new branch has today sprouted from this woman's loins, out of her blessed womb. The family is growing. And this baby will bring together our two families who've so long hated each other. Peace between brothers will be made.

ELECTRA

Mad, unconscious, and pregnant. You'd be better off if you had a abortion, mama, think about what the neighbors will say.

ORESTES

It's dangerous for a woman your age to have children.

ÆGISTHUS

Are you afraid something's going to be snatched away from you. Tell me honestly. Are you afraid of losing your money?

ELECTRA

Look at him: He's vomiting blood on his plate.

Pointing at empty place.

CLYTEMNESTRA

God you're spiteful! Here I am making love with the living, giving birth to new life, and you're doing it with the dead and giving birth to ghosts.

ELECTRA

He's weeping, look at him. You shouldn't have thrown this up at him, mama!

CLYTEMNESTRA

You want it to hate you before it's born?

ELECTRA

It'll be crippled and ugly and reek like a corpse.

ORESTES

It would be better if you had an abortion, mama.

ELECTRA

She's a whore.

ORESTES

Stop saying things that don't make sense.

ELECTRA

A whore who's turned this house into something filthy.

CLYTEMNESTRA

You talk like a hundred-year-old man. Some old, dead man. Your grandfather, your great-grandfather. Someone you've nursed in your gut too many years.

ELECTRA

It's my father speaking through me.

CLYTEMNESTRA

But you're a woman, Electra, like me, with breasts and a woman's organs.

ELECTRA

I'm not man or woman. I am the family.

CLYTEMNESTRA

And what are we?

ELECTRA

I hate her, Orestes, I hate her. She betrayed me. She betrayed me, you, all of us. Kill her!

> *Orestes takes a knife and kills his mother while the others quietly continue eating.*
>
> *Ægisthus and Clytemnestra on death beds surrounded with flowers.*

ELECTRA

How beautiful this mother of ours is, Orestes. Her eyelashes seem like wisps of gold. With her white lips, it seems she's ready to cry. But she won't cry. The knife cut deep in her breast. Her beautiful silk blouse is soaked with blood. I've always loved this mother. You remember when she was young, when she wore grandmother's dresses resewn to fit her. How awkward she was! And then ever since they cut open her stomach to take out her dead son, she always had chills and would bend in two with the pain. You remember how crazy she was at the hospital after the operation when all she wanted was ice cream and melons. And I'd eat ice cream and melons too, sitting on her bed with her. And then she'd say, 'Something's gnawing at my stomach,' and she'd vomit all aver the bed. 'When you're better, mama, we'll go to Spain,' I'd say. Who knows why Spain. I wanted to see Valencia and Castille. Somewhere I'd read how they were such white and graceful cities and that everyone danced as they walked. One day she gave me a package she wanted thrown in the ocean. I held onto that package for an entire day. I knew there was something in that package, something belonging to her, and maybe to me. Before throwing it away, I opened it and you know what I found? A tiny dead baby's body, all red and bloody. I threw it in the ocean after making the sign of the cross; how I loved this mother with her faults. When father would leave, when she'd put on her red print dress and would go off to her lover, the one with the huge hands, the sailor. How I loved her! She didn't love me; only Iphigenia – she loved, her delicate, fragile, always sickly, docile, starving baby. 'She needs attention because she's sick, she needs kisses, hugs, milk, sweets,' she'd say. And I'd go running up and down with my filthy smock for their disgusting pleasures. They'd kiss one another on the lips, they'd drink milk from mouth to mouth. My only consolation was him, my father, who looked like me, who loved me. But he wasn't around. He was so far away I couldn't manage even to dream about him. But I thought about him, I always thought about him with his tremendous body. Distant, silent, blind, how agonizing, while here she was, her skin reeking all over from the kitchen, with her body aches, her stomach aches, and me loving her and abusing her out of love, wanting to kill her, fixing her poisons. How I loved this mother, now that she's dead I love her even more. I could devour her bit by bit, piece by piece, her beauty I could swallow up. How it used to make me cry. You can't know how I loved her when she was young and painted red lipstick on her mouth. I'd paint myself too, on the sly. But on her lips it looked like geraniums, on mine new blood. I'd bite myself and take out my feelings with my teeth. But then she began to get old, with her flowing jet-black hair and I hated her because she was shriveling up like some over-ripe fruit, and she tell me I was the one making her get old: 'The more you grow up the older I get,' she'd say, biting into me. When I was thirteen she tried to strangle me, and I said to her, 'Mama, I want to be you, I want to be a geranium'. And she spit in my face and said I was a grown woman now, that I'd had my period, and she slapped me around so much that after I could barely open my mouth; how I loved this mother with her peasant arms. 'Here comes your father', she'd say, 'and he's going to kill you', and she'd pick up her skirt with that man with hands like giant's, in the boat, I saw them, I'd spy on them, he was my lover, not hers. She was so delicate and lovely with that beautiful body of hers that no one could seem to destroy. Then he'd beg on his knees to her and she'd laugh and piss in his mouth, and I'd die of jealousy, but my real heart was safe in my father's hands across the ocean, in a pistachio-colored Ford Escort, like he told me in a letter, 'I'll take you for a ride in the car to Siena' and I would have sent him my heart wrapped in flowered paper across the ocean and he would have had it as a token of my love. Before my watchful eyes she got old and got rich. All the way over there, my father in white pants and a white shirt, eating bread and honey and weeping because a father's commands are no longer obeyed, he sent me a telegram from the other side of the ocean saying: 'you're mine!' And I made up my mind for him. I dressed in black, I ate candy roses, I made every hair of my head like a snake to torture my faithless mother. Every day that went by was like a prison. The wait ate up my insides. Finally he came back and she murdered him. She gave me a package to throw in the river. Inside it was his head. But I didn't throw it away because the family comes before the future, before pleasure, before dreams, the family is him, his huge man's heart which never dies. How I loved this idiot mother who disobeyed all the paternal rules and now is dead and now I can tell her how she made me suffer from love and jealousy like no lover ever made me suffer. Weep with me Orestes. You carried yourself like a man. You struck justly. You avenged your father. Now you're a real man. You've become father, grandfather, and son. You're here. You're us. You won.

Orestes and Pilot in Milan.

PILOT

Did you get the bread?

ORESTES

Yes.

PILOT

Put it in the drawer. The water's on, see if it's boiling.

ORESTES

No.

PILOT

What's wrong?

ORESTES

Nothing.

PILOT

You've got a face down to the floor.

ORESTES

Leave me alone.

PILOT

Did something happen?

ORESTES

Nothing.

PILOT

See if the water's boiling.

Orestes doesn't answer, doesn't move.

Did you hear the election results? We won hands down. Just about everyone's a communist now in in this town. Even the office workers, the businessmen, and the doctors. A complete romp! Even everyone who's pilfering, cheating, and screwing the community. Now we'll see: will communism change the shitheads or will the shitheads change communism? What do you think? So, did you put the spaghetti in? No, naturally. You never lift a finger. It's always up to me. And what if I told you I was sick of cooking, cleaning, wiping your ass? Nothing to say? Sure, you don't feel well, you're depressed, you don't feel good about yourself – but why do I have to pay for your moods? I know you're suffering, but who knows from what; you have bad dreams, you see bloody ghosts everywhere, you keep going to the mailbox, poring over those barely legible letters from your crazy mother... What am I supposed to do with your problems? I don't give a shit ... you stupid ass ... what's bugging you? For a month now you're back and for a month you don't do bullshit; you're always tired, you make love like some robot, you wake up screaming, you tell me to go to hell, you eat like a pig and then for three days you eat nothing, you go to sleep when I have to get up and you get up when I have to sleep. I'm fed up, up to here. Your mother's sick, fine, so what? So you all shut her up in a mental hospital. So your old man killed himself. Fine. You all got your money back. Isn't that what you wanted? Him in a grave and her in some room, which isn't much different anyhow. You and Electra are big bosses, owners of a lovely textile plant in Prato, the town your parents chose for their new home; a total triumph. But you, goddamnit, go around like some sick dog with your tail between your legs. And I'm fucking tired of it, I'm not going to be part of your family, I don't give a flying fuck about your mother, your sister, or anything.

Orestes gets up.

Where are you going?

Orestes doesn't answer. He leaves.

Would you tell me where the fuck you're going? Look, if you're not back by eight I'm throwing you out. I'm tossing your stinking suitcases out the window. I'm not going to wait around for you, I'm not going to worry over you, I'm not your mother, understand!

Orestes at the tomb of his father (Aeschylus).

ORESTES

I've come to praise you, father, to weep for you:
And here before this tangled web of parricide
I tremble for my acts, my remorse,
here before my descendants. Of this victory
only the taste of death remains.
See, father, the Gorgons,
covered in black, with serpents
filling their hair ... I cannot hold back.
Specters repelling me, they are not,
this I know, but the furies of my mother!
From their eyes drips blood!
no one sees them but I see them
routing me, father, I find no rest.

He runs off.

MOIRA

(Aeschylus)

Three times through this house has blown
the tempest's fury:
The death of the children devoured
by Thyestes, was the first.
Then it was turn for the Greek army's
king to suffer,
murdered over an open tub.
And now for the third time
the wind sweeps through us. Yet is it hope
or despair? Where is it pointed?
Where will it scatter,
at last spent, death's song?

*Electra and Clytemnestra at the mental
hospital.*

ELECTRA

I brought you tangerines, mama.

CLYTEMNESTRA

Did you get laid, tell me, did you get laid?

ELECTRA

I took four sleeping pills.

CLYTEMNESTRA

I dreamed you made love with your brother.

ELECTRA

I got to sleep at five.

CLYTEMNESTRA

So was he good? Tell me about it.

ELECTRA

Orestes is in Milan with his friend, Pilot.

CLYTEMNESTRA

Those two I know are screwing around. The doctor, you know the one with the curly red hair, he's in love with me. But the nurse, the big fat one, is jealous, and is always right on his heels. I grabbed his hand and took it under my covers. She wanted to give me poison to punish me; so are we going to the movies together tomorrow?

ELECTRA

You can't move from here, mama. You're crazy. If you try and move, they'll tie you up.

CLYTEMNESTRA

I screamed all night long. They gave me an injection of morphine. But I can hear them, you know, chewing, chewing away. Did you see what incredible teeth they have? All night long they crunch on cookies. I started screaming and they twisted my arm. They don't want me to scream. The doctor put his dick in my hand. It was droopy and dead. I told him it was no big deal. He got furious. So, how many times did he come?

ELECTRA

The dead man?

CLYTEMNESTRA

Your father came only once. He sighed and fell asleep on my shoulder like a lamb. I should have kept up with my hands. You know what Orestes did with my nipples? He kept pulling and pulling at them till my breasts became so long they stretched out away from me; but it was always still me, even with my stretched-out skin going all the way past the door, and he'd put his feet on top of me, and I could feel the cold from the tiles on my skin. And I cried for pity for my breasts with all that moldy milk. You didn't tell me how many times he came.

ELECTRA

Four, mama.

CLYTEMNESTRA

I always said he was a lover. You know what I like? His mouth with those big curled-up lips. So nice. And then his hands. Did you see what a giant's hand he has. Here they'd put gloves on him. There's one guy who strangled his son a few months ago. They put yellow gloves on him and he goes around like this, in short-shorts and yellow gloves. Pus is always coming out of his fingers and they can't cure it. Every week his wife brings him a pair of new gloves. Either gray or yellow. So, how many times did he come?

ELECTRA

Mama, be good, or they'll tie you up. You know you have to be good. Here, have a tangerine. They're very sweet. You know how much I paid for them?

CLYTEMNESTRA

Your father was mad about those underpants with the opening in front. Those underpants were so airy I'd just stick in my hand and there he was, all ready. What a piece! Then he'd say, 'Listen, I'm leaving and I want you to stay faithful'. He'd say, 'put your hand here on my dick and swear. Make sure the next time you bring tangerines you throw them out the window. I could eat a whole goat, like back in your grandfather's days, with its big ugly jaw stuffed with myrtle, a smell that used to make your eyes tear, and it hissing all night on the fire, and once they even stuck it in me up to my neck. I screamed and he said, 'It is I who come back from the dead inside you.' They had me when I was fourteen, him with that woman of his with her head bandaged and his father, when his son was out, he came up to me and put his hands under my skirt, 'What does it matter now that everyone's had you,' he said, threatening me with a knife if I spoke, but he was gentle as can be and didn't hurt me at all; my son Orestes, that's how I got him, because deep down I didn't want an abortion. He's your grandfather's son.

ELECTRA

Like I told you, this time you had to have an abortion so you wouldn't give birth to some deformed, imbecile baby.

CLYTEMNESTRA

You didn't want an abortion the time I told you when you were pregnant from that asshole with the giant's hands. He was the only lover you ever had and I gave him to you, what a laugh! Does your stomach hurt?

ELECTRA

You were better off getting rid of that baby right away.

CLYTEMNESTRA

All lead-footed men. They crushed everything, they walked all over me, my breasts, my face. But then I never was able to do without the flesh. When he was fucking he'd curse out all the saints. Who knows if that's what he did too with that American girl with the long. long hair, what was her name?

ELECTRA

Cassandra.

CLYTEMNESTRA

She was nice. We made friends. Then from one day to the next she was gone. What a jerk! We could have done big things together. You know who I like too? That skinny, skinny orderly with the mustache; he looks just barely twenty, did you see how gorgeous he is?

ELECTRA

Nobody wants you anymore, mama. Your skin is sagging and your teeth are black.

CLYTEMNESTRA

I know someone who went up his ass with his fist. And there was no shit up his ass; he smelled like roses; he was a gorgeous boy; he kept coming to me in my dreams, but then he disappeared. He had a beard like Jesus and a tiny, tiny dick. You think I'll ever get out of here?

ELECTRA

I don't think so.

CLYTEMNESTRA

They locked me up here to take me out of circulation. They think I don't know it. I pretend to be crazy to keep them happy. But I can see it all. They're measuring my sex drive here. Are you measuring it?

ELECTRA

You made a disgrace of yourself, mama. You were undressing in the streets, throwing yourself at any man who came by. Your language got filthy. Everyone complained about you in the neighborhood, you know it.

CLYTEMNESTRA

If your left hand disgraces you, cut it off with your right.

ELECTRA

You made a disgrace of yourself, mama.

CLYTEMNESTRA

Disgrace is my pride and joy. Someone has to make a disgrace of themselves, don't you know?

ELECTRA

Everyone in the neighborhood complained.

CLYTEMNESTRA

This man comes to me and says, 'Lady, there's a young boy outside who wants to see you.' And I say, 'Let him in.' I put on that geranium red lipstick you love, and with that taste of flowers on my lips, I wait for him. This tiny little boy comes in, who I wouldn't have even noticed, all washed out with crooked teeth and this mousy face. Right away I opened his pants and saw what I'd suspected: He had this huge snake with a head covered with dancing stars. I'd whistle and he danced. And that's how I got him on the bed and I made him eat his heart out.

ELECTRA

Crazy, sick dreams, mama. You stink like some dead animal, you're all wrinkled and you're ugly.

CLYTEMNESTRA

There was a sister of charity who used to wash me in a tiny little tub; she'd wash me all over with warm water, hair by hair, inch by inch. She was so gentle. But then when she fell in love with me they sent her to Sardinia. She left me her address. I'm going to give it to you and I want you to send her a card from me. She wore a black veil that smelled like fried grease, but I've never felt anything like her fingers, they were so light, like butterflies.

ELECTRA

All you think of are filthy things, mama. You're crazy, a crazy lunatic with sex on the brain. Now it's time to just stop it. You're a disgrace. You've always been a disgrace. Instead of staying nice and quiet in your husband's house, you go running around the neighborhood, offending the neighbor's sensibilities. Just think a little about death and what's waiting for you.

CLYTEMNESTRA

I'm already dead, you think I don't know it. But even the dead play games and holler about sex. You want to hear what my cunt says?

ELECTRA

I don't want to hear any of your filth. You've tortured me enough. Why don't you be good just a little bit, like all the other mothers in the world – quiet, peaceful, doing your housework, waiting for your children and husband. But then I suppose that would be asking you to be someone else.

CLYTEMNESTRA

Yes, you're right. I'll be good. Can I have tangerine? If you knew how good I was when I went around the streets at thirteen. I'd always say yes. And for a piece of bread or cheese I'd give all of myself. If someone hurt me I wouldn't say boo so as not to offend. And whatever they gave me, even if it was only five lire or a paper plate with fried fish, I'd thank them a million times over. I had no rights and all it took was one foot to squash me. Your father put me to work as the maid for him and that beautiful girl with the bandaged head and I'd always thank them and thank them; it seemed like a miracle there was someone who didn't spit at me or kick me.

ELECTRA

You should still be thanking him. He took you off the street, you said so; he gave you a name and a family. But you cheated him, hated him, and killed him.

CLYTEMNESTRA

You should see how beautiful he is without a shirt, not one hair, with skin soft as a feather. His dick would just about fly away from him; that's why I held it with two hands. And I'd swallow it whole. 'Now I'm bringing you to the graveyard,' he'd say, 'as a gravedigger I must do what I must,' and I'd say, 'No, please, let me eat you some more you're so gorgeous!' But just then the nun came in and threw him against the wall and nailed him to the cross that's still up there; see how much blood the poor man lost? It was the nun from the third floor; she's killed so many I've lost track; my poor sweetheart, you never get laid, are you frigid?

Moira and Clytemnestra (citing Aeschylus).

MOIRA

Oh, wretched women! companions,
what torment!
what useless torment!
An unspeakable anxiety
torments us; an evil
impossible to bear!

CLYTEMNESTRA

Again the obsessive song,
vertigo lost
to reason, the hymn
of the Furies
imprisoning the soul
voice without instrument
empty of life.

MOIRA

Awake and wake the others as I wake you.
Do you sleep? Do not sleep!
Brace yourself against sleep.
What truth is there to this nightmare?

CLYTEMNESTRA

Stricken I lie in the depths of my dreams,
A whip-lash breaking
my heart, my spirit:
A feeling of nausea
overcomes me preceding
the executioner's brutal blow.

MOIRA

Join us round in chorus,
The time is nigh to cry out
our desperate song,
to announce the dispersal
of our presence among men!

Orestes and Moira on the street.

ORESTES

You mind if I sit here for a minute?

MOIRA

Want to suck my tongue?

ORESTES

My feet are killing me.

MOIRA

Relax.

ORESTES

I can't. I feel sick if I sit still.

MOIRA

Can you spare a few bucks?

ORESTES

All I asked was a minute to relax. I don't want your body.

MOIRA

Want to suck my tongue?

ORESTES

I don't go for women.

MOIRA

Not even me? I'm thirteen. With amazing breasts. Want to see?

ORESTES

Take a look at me: I don't exist. I talk and walk. But you can see right through me. I'm not here.

MOIRA

Haven't you got anything to eat in your bag?

ORESTES

Where have I seen you before?

MOIRA

In a dream.

ORESTES

A thousand years ago.

MOIRA

Want to suck my tongue?

ORESTES

I told you, no? I don't feel well, get it. All I have left is my will. Which is what keeps me going.

MOIRA

Haven't you got anything to eat in your bag?

ORESTES

Where'd you get so beat up and ugly looking?

MOIRA

In the reformatory.

ORESTES

You run away?

MOIRA

I've got amazing breasts, want to see?

ORESTES

So you hang out on the streets. Where do you sleep?

MOIRA

Wherever I can.

ORESTES

And sell yourself for nothing. You're a dope. Settle on a good price and charge the shit out of those fucking assholes who buy you. No price is enough for a child's body like yours.

MOIRA

Want to suck my tongue?

ORESTES

I don't go for women.

MOIRA

I'm thirteen. With amazing breasts. Want to see?

ORESTES

No.

MOIRA

Haven't you got anything to eat in your bag?

ORESTES

No.

MOIRA

Want my shoes?

ORESTES

Your feet are very big. All the same, they wouldn't
fit me. Shoes last me three days. Every three days
I buy a new pair of shoes. It's a curse.

MOIRA

You have much money?

ORESTES

I would ...

MOIRA

Want to suck my tongue?

ORESTES

I don't go for women.

MOIRA

But you do for me, you like me. I've got great
breasts, want to see?

ORESTES

I like you because you're a child. But how did
you ever get such big feet with such a tiny, little
body?

MOIRA

My mother had big feet.

ORESTES

It's seven years since I made love with a woman.
Want to do it with me?

MOIRA

You've got to have something to eat in that bag,
no?

ORESTES

I know I've heard your voice somewhere before,
but where?

MOIRA

In a dream.

ORESTES

A thousand years ago.

MOIRA

Want to see my breasts or my legs first?

ORESTES

Don't talk to me that way. Just shut up. I'm your
lover. I'm good-looking and didn't come here,
you know, to make an exchange, but for love; I
love you very much and don't want to just take
you; you're going to take me, right here on the
ground, under this tree; I want to get lost in you,
disappear; I want your body to swallow me up,
how about it? Tell me you want me, take me,
love, take me!

The two embrace and roll around the ground. At a certain moment he takes one of her stockings and strangles her. Blackout. When the lights go up, three women stand next to his sleeping body. Moira is gone.

FIRST WOMAN

It's him.

SECOND WOMAN

I recognize him.

THIRD WOMAN

Kick him in the mouth.

FIRST WOMAN

And again and again, in his face, in his balls.

SECOND WOMAN

That's not enough.

THIRD WOMAN

We'll stone him.

FIRST WOMAN

Smashing in his head is too easy.

SECOND WOMAN

We'll drag his heart out his ass.

THIRD WOMAN

We'll gnaw him into a million bits.

FIRST WOMAN

We'll tear him to pieces.

THIRD WOMAN

First I want to hear what he has to say.

SECOND WOMAN

We'll put him on the stand.

THIRD WOMAN

Yes, on trial.

FIRST WOMAN

Then he'll have to talk.

SECOND WOMAN

Hey, you!

She shakes him with a kick.

ORESTES

What do you want, you gross pigs!

The three old women si down together on one side in front of him.

FIRST WOMAN

What's with you, tell us!

ORESTES

I can't say anything. I have to go.

SECOND WOMAN

No, you're staying here.

ORESTES

What do you want with me?

THIRD WOMAN

How about you tell us what you did last night?

ORESTES

I can't. I'm tired. I have to get going. They're waiting for me.

FIRST WOMAN

Open that shit mouth of yours and tell us the truth.

ORESTES

I didn't do anything that's any of your business.

SECOND WOMAN

What do you know about what is and what's not our business?

ORESTES

I don't know you. I didn't do anything to you.

THIRD WOMAN

He didn't do anything. So he's innocent. Are you innocent?

ORESTES

What I did has only to do with me, not you.

FIRST WOMAN

No, you're wrong. It is our business.

SECOND WOMAN

Take off your shirt, boy!

ORESTES

I'm not taking anything off.

THIRD WOMAN

Strip, you worm.

ORESTES

What for?

FIRST WOMAN

You show up naked in court, don't you know?

ORESTES

What court?

SECOND WOMAN

Ours.

THIRD WOMAN

Strip. We've got knives and we're stronger than
you.

ORESTES

All right, I'll strip. But I don't get it.

FIRST WOMAN

Now answer us: where were you last night?

ORESTES

I don't know. I've been wandering around for
days. I don't know where I am. I fell asleep.

SECOND WOMAN

But first, what did you do?

ORESTES

I made love with a woman.

THIRD WOMAN

And what was the woman's name?

ORESTES

I don't know.

THIRD WOMAN

Her name was Moira. And she was thirteen years
old.

ORESTES

Yes, I know, she told me. But it wasn't the first time she made love. She began when she was ten. She was already corrupted, already lost. I wasn't the one to take her virginity. And on top of it, she wanted it herself.

SECOND WOMAN

So you maintain you're innocent?

ORESTES

Look, what do you want from me, you old bags?

THIRD WOMAN

And afterwards, what did you do after?

ORESTES

Nothing. I fell asleep.

FIRST WOMAN

He's looking to rile us.

SECOND WOMAN

And who strangled the girl, according to you .

ORESTES

How should I know. It must have been someone who came after me.

SECOND WOMAN

No one came after you.

THIRD WOMAN

Since you're not getting out of here alive anyhow, just tell us the truth.

ORESTES

I'm a worker. I was an immigrant in Germany. I suffered huger, cold, racism. I've been exploited just like you.

FIRST WOMAN

So are you going to strip or not?

ORESTES

All right, I'll strip. But I didn't do anything. Take me to the police.

SECOND WOMAN

Sure, so you can get two years and a kick in the ass for killing a prostitute.

THIRD WOMAN

Killing one of us is nothing.

FIRST WOMAN

Us, we're the plague.

SECOND WOMAN

We carry diseases.

THIRD WOMAN

When you kill us you do them a favor.

FIRST WOMAN

You're the one.

ORESTES

Hand me over to the police. I want a fair trial.
Who are you all? When did old prostitutes start
being judges? What do you know about the law,
the rules, justice?

SECOND WOMAN

We know enough to judge you guilty.

ORESTES

I never did anything bad. Ever. Only today, I
admit, I had one moment of insanity, one slip.
I lost my head. I got drunk going into her,
feeling deep in her body. There I was so tiny, lost
inside her, in the dark, in her enormous dark
body, and she was swallowing me, crushing me,
drinking me up. I got afraid and started shaking.
I wanted to go but she wouldn't let me. She kept
sucking and sucking away at me, making me
disappear inside her. I killed her to get free; she
wanted to kill me. It was just self-defense. Just
self-defense.

FIRST WOMAN

Death is a small price for you.

ORESTES

I killed her by accident, in self defense, take me to the police.

FIRST WOMAN

Now get up, murderer, and lean against that wall. We condemn you to being skinned alive.

ORESTES

I didn't do anything, I didn't do anything!

Orestes wakes up screaming. The three women disappear.

ORESTES

Moira, Moira! where are you?

MOIRA

Right here, what is it?

ORESTES

I has a terrible dream.

MOIRA

You were raving in your sleep.

ORESTES

Give me your hand. You're still alive. Forgive me! I dreamed I killed you.

MOIRA

How?

ORESTES

Strangled.

MOIRA

You tried to last night while we were making love, but you weren't strong enough.

ORESTES

Then I was sleeping the whole time?

MOIRA

So how much are you giving me?

ORESTES

I'll give you everything I have.

MOIRA

How much?

ORESTES

Twenty thousand lire.

MOIRA

All for me?

ORESTES

Yes, all for you. Forgive me if I hurt you.

MOIRA

Give me the money.

Orestes gives her the money in thousand-lire bills. Moira counts them one by one.

Thanks.

ORESTES

You happy?

MOIRA

Yes.

ORESTES

So long.

MOIRA

Want to suck my tongue?

ORESTES

I can't breathe when I stay put. You saw what a nightmare I had when I stayed here with you. I have to go.

MOIRA

So long.

ORESTES

So long.

He goes.

Electra and Clytemnestra in the mental hospital.

ELECTRA

Orestes got married. I brought you some of the confetti.

CLYTEMNESTRA

I dreamed I made love with him. I was thirteen. I'd just run away from the reformatory. He started shouting something I don't know and strangled me. Don't dead people have real desires?

ELECTRA

Don't you want to know your son got married?

CLYTEMNESTRA

He was very sweet and gentle. He said he wanted to go deep inside me. Then he got furious. He started grabbing me by the neck.

ELECTRA

She's a beautiful girl from Milan. One of those fashion models.

CLYTEMNESTRA

He couldn't get to sleep.

ELECTRA

He looks good. He's happy. He's dropped that disgusting Pilot. He's a normal man now.

CLYTEMNESTRA

He wanted to kill himself.

ELECTRA

A year ago. Then he got professional help. You know, he looks younger. He's very handsome. I never realized how handsome he was. He lost it the minute he left for Germany. He's even put on some weight. He's extremely handsome.

CLYTEMNESTRA

He wanted to die.

ELECTRA

He's started up a whole little business: He's rented a huge workspace and bought ten new looms, and taken on all sorts of workers. He has her doing the office work. It seems she's good at keeping the books.

CLYTEMNESTRA

Once he was sitting on my knees and I took his dick in my hand and asked him. 'What are you doing to do with this when you grow up, my love?' And he said, 'Mama, I'm saving it all for you.' Then he wanted to die.

296

ELECTRA

He's bought two Ford delivery trucks and goes all over Prato buying and selling.

CLYTEMNESTRA

Once he told me, 'Mama, take me back inside you?' I told him, 'When you're grown up you can come back inside me.' Then he wanted to die.

ELECTRA

They say she had more lovers than you could count with your hands and feet together; she fought with everyone; she even smashed her father in the head with a hammer when he wanted to make her stay home. But with Orestes, of course, she's completely good.

CLYTEMNESTRA

Once he told me, 'Mama, can I have a little milk?' So I say, 'Yes, my love, it's in the refrigerator.' Then he ripped open my blouse, grabbed my tit and put it in his mouth. 'It's this milk I want, mama,' he said.

ELECTRA

You know what he did? He completely fixed up the house. He had two more rooms built over the roof. He fixed up the kitchen, you remember how terrible it was? He had another bathroom built. And the whole place was painted, completely clean; it seems like new.

CLYTEMNESTRA

He had a short, thick dick. Once I told him, 'Why doesn't your dick ever get bigger?' And he says, 'Because it gets wider.' In fact, his dick is wider than it is long. A real rarity. Have you ever seen a dick like his?

ELECTRA

He bought himself a new car, a pistachio-colored Ford Escort. She dresses very well, she looks like some royalty. She's tall, you know, and blond; she looks like a statue.

CLYTEMNESTRA

Once he told me, 'What would happen if you and I got married?' I said, 'Nothing would happen, my love, but you wouldn't be happy because it's a sin.' And you know what he answered me? 'Mama, I like not being happy. I feel good when I'm not happy.'

Enter three nurses.

FIRST NURSE

It's time to sleep.

SECOND NURSE

And close the window.

THIRD NURSE

And say your prayers.

FIRST NURSE

Who are you?

ELECTRA

Her daughter.

SECOND NURSE

Go home. The patient has to sleep.

ELECTRA

Bye, mama. I'll cry for you tomorrow if you're dead.

CLYTEMNESTRA

I'm in love, I can't go yet.

ELECTRA

Think about more serious things.

She goes.

FIRST NURSE

Did you brush your teeth?

CLYTEMNESTRA

No.

SECOND NURSE

Did you go to the bathroom?

CLYTEMNESTRA

No.

THIRD NURSE

Have you thought about God?

CLYTEMNESTRA

No.

THIRD NURSE

Have you wanted to die?

CLYTEMNESTRA

No.

SECOND NURSE

Did you play with yourself?

CLYTEMNESTRA

Yes.

FIRST NURSE

We'll give her an injection to tranquilize her.

SECOND NURSE

If you keep on playing with yourself and using foul language, we'll take you in for electroshock treatments.

CLYTEMNESTRA

Take your electroshock and shove it. Even if God himself came down I wouldn't stop it.

THIRD NURSE

Now be good or we'll tie you up for the night.

CLYTEMNESTRA

If you tie me up, I'll scream.

FIRST NURSE

Be good, be good.

She screams. They beat her. The psychoanalyst arrives.

PSYCHOANALYST

What's going on here?

SECOND NURSE

She doesn't want us tying her up.

PSYCHOANALYST

Leave. And close the door. I'll handle it.

The nurses leave.

PSYCHOANALYST

So, Clytemnestra, what's wrong?

CLYTEMNESTRA

When did that dick of yours last pop out of your underwear, Mr. Psychoanalyst?

PSYCHOANALYST

We're talking about you, not me.

CLYTEMNESTRA

Is that forbidden?

PSYCHOANALYST

My life is pretty boring and everyday – not very interesting. You, on the other hand, have lots of things to tell us, no?

CLYTEMNESTRA

A very nice way of telling me I'm crazy. But I don't give a fuck about you or me. I want you to untie me.

PSYCHOANALYST

Your psyche, Clytemnestra, is sweet and pure. I know all about you. I know that behind your anger there's a great need for affection. It's only that you feel you have to play a particular role.

CLYTEMNESTRA

If you give me more electroshock treatments, I'll kill myself.

PSYCHOANALYST

You are very free and poetic person; you're both clever and intelligent. Now I just don't understand why you keep insisting on playing out the role of a rebel.

CLYTEMNESTRA

Your dick gets as excited as anyone's, look at me. I saw it swell up plenty when you had that naked screaming girl in your hands.

PSYCHOANALYST

You'd like to provoke me, I know. But it's not all that easy, Clytemnestra; you see while you're playing I'm working.

CLYTEMNESTRA

You were born out of your father's head.

PSYCHOANALYST

I know the value of peaceful relations and I'm not going to preach morals to you. I wouldn't even know about morals. I'm simply asking you in the name of peaceful relations, of everyone's happiness.

CLYTEMNESTRA

You, you never knew your mother.

PSYCHOANALYST

This rebellion of yours is simply sterile, a losing battle. If you're good, if you learn to clean up your speech, and respect others, and do what the doctor tells you, you'll get out. You're an educated, intelligent, capable woman, and I'm sure you'd find work easily.

CLYTEMNESTRA

Why don't you stick me with that blackmailing dick of yours, psychoanalyst, just once, how about it?

PSYCHOANALYST

The others are not like you. The others understand and know how to carry themselves. They're not out-of-hand and obsessive as you are. The nurses are happy. And everything runs smoothly.

CLYTEMNESTRA

I do what the fuck I want.

PSYCHOANALYST

Your aggressiveness ... well ... I could give a whole lecture on your aggressiveness ... Your aggressiveness, your filthy language, your sexual obsession, your infantile exhibitionism – you know what they all are? Envy pure and simple, envy of a man's virility. You don't accept the feminine part of yourself, your gentleness, your passivity. You're looking to reevaluate yourself in terms of men and power and you end up bitter and hysterical.

CLYTEMNESTRA

I'll be waiting for you tonight, my psychoanalyst, with your big, rising dick. Come along and we'll have a blast.

PSYCHOANALYST

You want me to tie you up?

CLYTEMNESTRA

I already am; didn't you notice, you piece of shit?

PSYCHOANALYST

But these are gentle restraints. It could be much worse. Here in your bed you've got people around taking care of you. You have yet to experience the detention bed in the closed room.

CLYTEMNESTRA

I know about it. An old lady who used to share my room died there. Did anyone ever tell you you have beautiful eyes, psychoanalyst!

PSYCHOANALYST

As a child you're very taken with your own body, which is natural: You're learning to know it. As a child you masturbate and become passionate and aggressive, which is natural because you're discovering your femininity. Your own world is not much different from the masculine one: The center of your sexuality is your clitoris, and your attitude is hostile. But then, here we are, as you grow up, you become a woman and you transfer your feelings of pleasure from the external to the internal, learning to be receptive, docile, maternal. You become a woman. This is the pattern of a healthily matured femininity. You on the other hand ... you, you have remained a child – aggressive, hostile, and clitoris-centered. And this is what is making you crazy. The conflict was never resolved in you. The conflict of baby Clytemnestra has stayed alive in you and is destroying your fiber.

CLYTEMNESTRA

I love your thighs. Even if you didn't have a dick it wouldn't matter. You've got a great ass. Why don't you come here in my bed?

PSYCHOANALYST

A clear case of obstinacy defined by paranoia. How many electroshock treatments have we given you?

CLYTEMNESTRA

I'd stroke you like nobody ever has. How about it? First just untie me, if not how am I going to stroke you.

PSYCHOANALYST

Manic regression. Expulsionary schizophrenia.
I don't know if it can be reversed. I just don't
frankly know. It could take up to three years of
analysis and another twenty, thirty more
electroshock sessions. You're intelligent, Clytemnestra, and you can speak well. Why don't
you just think about it a minute? In your own
interest you'd do well to get better, leave here
and become normal woman. You could do a
world of things. All you want is to be loved. But
then you do everything to provoke hate. Just as
children do.

CLYTEMNESTRA

Want to suck my tongue?

PSYCHOANALYST

You had an unhappy childhood. You were raped,
sold and hated. Now you're getting back. But
what's the use? You really ought to try to be an
adult, Clytemnestra, adult and happy, you have
a world of possibilities.

CLYTEMNESTRA

I'd love to lick your eyes. Let me lick your eyes!

PSYCHOANALYST

Now, that's enough. The others have to sleep.
Only a thin wall is separating you from the

general room. You've made enough trouble. You've kept everyone from sleeping, or having good dreams. We can't even put anyone in here with you because of the filthy things you say and do. If you're not good, you're getting electro-shock treatments, and you better know it. I'll be back in the morning!

> *Alone by herself, Clytemnestra sings to keep herself company. Enter the three old prostitutes.*

THIRD WOMAN

God will forgive you.

SECOND WOMAN

God will have pity on you.

CLYTEMNESTRA

You've all betrayed me.

THIRD WOMAN

God will dry your salty cheeks.

FIRST WOMAN

God will kiss your tired lips.

SECOND WOMAN

We are the unclean servants of his virile glory.

CLYTEMNESTRA

You've all betrayed me. You let the murderer go.
They let him off.

THIRD WOMAN

It's science that changed us.

FIRST WOMAN

We are the shit that drops from the ass of God.

SECOND WOMAN

We are the women of hell, shut up in the house
of paradise, for our purification and glory.

THIRD WOMAN

We are the diamond in the divine viscera.

CLYTEMNESTRA

You sold yourselves to God for a little peace and
glory.

FIRST WOMAN

We were converted by democratic logic

CLYTEMNESTRA

You, the daughters of the night.

SECOND WOMAN

We were converted by the greased finger of a
masculine divinity.

CLYTEMNESTRA

You who carried the plague in your blood.

THIRD WOMAN

We were domesticated for the peaceful relations of men and women.

CLYTEMNESTRA

You who defended the cause of women carrying epidemics to men.

FIRST WOMAN

For this we do penance licking the floor of God's house.

CLYTEMNESTRA

Wake me if I'm sleeping, put me to sleep if I'm awake.

SECOND WOMAN

We were all tied up.

FIRST WOMAN

Torn to pieces.

CLYTEMNESTRA

You, the futures from the coralline lips!

THIRD WOMAN

We've been reborn benign.

FIRST WOMAN

We lost our fury as an outdated illness.

CLYTEMNESTRA

You were afraid.

SECOND WOMAN

Now we're happy.

THIRD WOMAN

We stink of happiness.

FIRST WOMAN

Frozen with joy.

SECOND WOMAN

Livid with pleasure.

CLYTEMNESTRA

You sold yourselves out of fear.

THIRD WOMAN

We've come to bring you recent news.

FIRST WOMAN

It was decided that killing an adulterous mother is not an unpardonable crime.

SECOND WOMAN

It was decided that man is born from a father's seed.

THIRD WOMAN

It was decided that the mother is only a recipient.

SECOND WOMAN

Justice has passed into the hands of the keepers of paternal law.

THIRD WOMAN

Calm has returned.

FIRST WOMAN

Sleep has returned.

SECOND WOMAN

The bitch was barking too much.

THIRD WOMAN

The epidemic in town has been overcome.

FIRST WOMAN

I, the ancient sage.

SECOND WOMAN

I, the infinite sadness, dry of tears.

THIRD WOMAN

I, woman's fate, drugged with sleeping pills.

FIRST WOMAN

With tranquilizers.

THIRD WOMAN

Now I smile quietly and peacefully.

CLYTEMNESTRA

Oh mother night, the betrayal is complete.

FIRST WOMAN

What torment pierces my side?

SECOND WOMAN

What horror penetrates my heart?

FIRST WOMAN

We are subjugated.

SECOND WOMAN

Worn out.

FIRST WOMAN

Faithful servants of the father.

SECOND WOMAN

Take me, God.

THIRD WOMAN

Kiss me, God.

FIRST WOMAN

Give me a sign, God, without you I do not exist.

The three women disappear.

CLYTEMNESTRA

I was dreaming. I am dreaming. My hands are smeared with my poisonous dreams. I dreamed I was me. I dreamed I was another. Between the two dreams there's no connection. Dreams give me strength. Dreams take away my strength. Women of my dreams, don't betray me, help me! Can a dead woman dream she's living again while dreaming her most mutilated dreams? Maybe now the hour of death has come, as my daughter Electra wanted, in the name of truth and family order. If I die dreaming possibly I'll die happy. And yet is that a dream of life or a life of dreaming? Somewhere, among dead dreams, I will keep on living, to keep on dreaming.

Clytemnestra dies.

MOIRA

Citing Æschylus.

Miserable, degraded me!
Oh, to men will I bear
my sorrow, my anger!
Every fallen drop
from my heart
for you will be poison: And a leprous sore
on his sons will spread justice and
all will be only a rotting wound.
Here I weep, and yet I must act.

This city must I lay now!
Oh, how they have suffered,
how the have suffered, unhappy daughters
of the night, daughters all wounded!

END

Crime at the Tennis Club

Freely adapted from a short story
by Alberto Moravia.

Translated by
Tony Mitchell.

On Title page: Maddelena Troupe performing in streets of Rome in 1978.

Preface

This short play is based on a short story by the Italian novelist Alberto Moravia, entitled *Crime at the Tennis Club.* Moravia was an important early influence on Maraini's work. Together with filmmaker Pier Paolo Pasolini and others, Moravia and Maraini founded the Teatro Porscopino in Rome in 1967. Maraini and Moravia lived together for 18 years and remained friends until his death in 1991. She also wrote a book about Moravia's early childhood, entitled *Il bambino Alberto,* published in 1987. Maraini has been critical of Moravia's attitude towards women and the female body, as reflected in his writings. For her, his portraits of women often appear cruel.

In both the Moravia short story and the Maraini play, the central character is an old woman, who is killed by three young men. In the Moravia tale, 'La principessa' (the Princess) is portrayed as a stupid, vain, ridiculous old woman who still wants to be beautiful and sexy. She enjoys the teasing of the young men, who mock her vanity. She is thereby, in a way, a victim of her own needfulness, and a co-conspirator in their cruelty. 'I was struck by the cruelty of the gaze directed at the woman's body,' Maraini has said of Moravia's story. In Maraini's play, the point of view is that of 'La principessa,' who is a strong woman, good-natured and a bit naive, but clearly undeserving of her tragic fate. She plays the youths' game when they tease her, in an attempt to understand them, probably because her own son has died. She does become aware of their violence, but their killing of her is portrayed as a kind of accident.

Moravia's story tells us very little about the male characters who commit this gang murder. But Maraini, in her play, creates through the male dialogue 'a world of fathers and sons in continual conflict,' a hatred by sons of their fathers' bourgeois values, and a pervasive spirit of resentment and meanness. In her notes for the play's 1988 performance in Rome, Maraini wrote:

> 'The Princess speaks a totally different language, which seems to come from different times and different emotions. Her experience as a mother has taught her that sons can be brutal, sordid, and nasty, but they stop miraculously short of murder when they are confronted by the fear of losing the person whose lot is always to look after their interests ... [Hence] she does not notice the violence that is building up and seeking a devastating release. By the time she realizes her body is the

object of this violence it is too late ...'

Subsequently she has written:

'What constitutes an element of surprise in the play is the indifference of the young men after the murder of the Princess, as if nothing serious had taken place. But it is precisely this indifference that shows the horror of the situation, by revealing the violence which is experienced in certain social milieux as right and privilege, part of a game in which the man is the hunter and the woman is the prey.'

'Crime At the Tennis Club' was first performed in Rome in 1988, directed by Ugo Margio. This is a first translation into English by Tony Mitchell.

Crime at the Tennis Club

Characters

The Princess
a woman of 60

Ripandelli
a young man of 35

Costa
a man about 40

Micheli
a man between 30 and 40

Lucini
a young man of 30

Setting

A side room containing a sofa covered with coats.
A large glass door behind which people can be
seen at a party. Lights and shadows.

Period

Late 1950s

The four men are sitting at a table playing cards.

RIPANDELLI

I pass.

LUCINI

Pass.

MICHELI

Both of you?

RIPANDELLI

More winnings for you.

LUCINI

To Costa.

Are you passing too?

COSTA

Yeah, I pass.

LUCINI

To Micheli.

How about you?

MICHELI

Looks like I'm playing against myself. I had two pairs too, damn it.

RIPANDELLI

Two pairs? Is that all?

RIPANDELLI

Whose deal is it?

MICHELI

Mine.

RIPANDELLI

Here, you bullshitter.

MICHELI

Look who's talking. You can talk more bullshit in an hour than I can in a week.

Micheli deals the cards.

RIPANDELLI

Bullshitting is an art form. Not everybody has a gift for it.

COSTA

You know what a crapshooter is?

RIPANDELLI

Someone who shoots crap.

COSTA

And what sort of crap do you shoot?

RIPANDELLI

The sort of crap you shoot in a crap game.

COSTA

Crap, crape, crappie, craps, crapshooter ...

RIPANDELLI

Stop crapping on about crap and get on with it.

MICHELI

Yeah, let's get on with it.

RIPANDELLI

Only aces and face cards, right?

MICHELI

Fine by me.

LUCINI

O.K.

COSTA

Me too.

MICHELI

Ready?

RIPANDELLI

Right.

MICHELI

How many cards?

RIPANDELLI

Three for me.

COSTA

One.

LUCINI

I'll stick with mine.

RIPANDELLI

You're bluffing.

LUCINI

Sure I'm bluffing.

MICHELI

Two for me.

Shouts are heard from the next room.

LUCINI

What's going on in there?

RIPANDELLI

They must be slaughtering the pig.

LUCINI

What pig?

RIPANDELLI

There's plenty to choose from – your father, my father, could be anyone!

LUCINI

My father's a respectable citizen.

RIPANDELLI

Oh, so is mine, don't get me wrong. Respectable citizens make the best pigs.

MICHELI

Sounds like an orgy to me.

COSTA

Our fathers and mothers are all respectable senior citizens. How could they be having an orgy?

MICHELI

Mummies are good dancers, you know. Whenever I go to sleep I see a white room full of hundreds of dancing mummies. I'm the only one who isn't mummified. After a while I get tired and have to stop, but they just carry on dancing. I collapse on the floor in the middle of the room and watch them prancing about for hours on end, all wrapped up in their winding sheets. What do you think this dream means?

RIPANDELLI

It means you're a total idiot.

COSTA

Old people used to have second childhoods. Now they have second adolescences. The older they get, the younger they get. It's tragic.

MICHELI

Anyone who lives to the age of seventy should have the decency to commit suicide.

LUCINI

Sure, and let young pups like you take over.

MICHELI

Who are you calling a pup?

RIPANDELLI

He's more like a leech.

MICHELI

Yeah, leech suits him.

RIPANDELLI

Yeah, I've got really good at leeching off my family. I'm so cool they don't even notice me sucking their blood any more.

Laughs.

COSTA

O.K., what are we playing for?

MICHELI

I'll raise it thirty.

RIPANDELLI

Is that all? I'll see you.

LUCINI

Me too.

COSTA

I'm out. Bloody useless cards.

MICHELI

Right.

Shows his cards.

Full house, how about that? And you thought I was bluffing.

RIPANDELLI

It was written all over your face.

MICHELI

What was?

RIPANDELLI

Your stupidity.

MICHELI

You're a bad looser, Ripa. You asshole.

RIPANDELLI

Asshole is O.K. I'm a connoisseur of asses. I like sniffing out a piece of ass – I'm a real bloodhound.

MICHELI

So asshole is a compliment, and idiot an insult?

RIPANDELLI

Sure. Asshole comes from 'our soul', people with soul. Idiot comes from *I-dio,* meaning God, which is dog in reverse. Idiots are people who believe in God, or anything else for that matter.

MICHELI

Such as?

RIPANDELLI

Religion, politics, any kind of mystery.

COSTA

They stink too.

RIPANDELLI

Yeah, they stink of stale dog.

COSTA

More like stale sweat and unmade beds, and collapsed lungs.

MICHELI

For God's sake, can we get on with the game?

RIPANDELLI

We always get back to God. What do you reckon, if that door opened and in he came in green gumboots and a flowery waistcoat, would he have a commie red scarf round his neck?

LUCINI

Stop blaspheming. I happen to be a Catholic.

RIPANDELLI

What sort of Catholic?

LUCINI

Just a Catholic. No special sort.

MICHELI

To Lucini

We're all Catholics in that case.

RIPANDELLI

Do you believe in hell, then?

LUCINI

Sure I do. You mean you don't?

RIPANDELLI

Don't worry, I do ... The flames of corruption, the grapes of wrath, the joys of gluttony, the quiverings of lust – hell is the only place to be.

COSTA

We'd be a lot better off if hell wasn't crowded out by our parents.

Shouts and laughter are heard.

MICHELI

They sound like they're tearing each other apart.

COSTA

They're not tearing each other apart, they're having a good time. They're octagonals.

LUCINI

Octagonals? What the hell are you talking about?

COSTA

They've got octagonal brains instead of round ones. Old people are weirder than you think.

RIPANDELLI

A different species.

MICHELI

Yeah, aliens.

RIPANDELLI

No one's sure if they're higher or lower forms of life, but they're definitely aliens.

COSTA

Definitely different.

MICHELI

Are we still playing, or what?

COSTA

No, thanks. I can't concentrate with all that yelling in there.

MICHELI

Want to go and check out the action?

COSTA

What action? Stapled-up stomachs, tucked-up cheeks and eyes held open with matchsticks?

RIPANDELLI

They hold things up and we have to hold things down.

COSTA

They cover things up, we discover them.

RIPANDELLI

They eat, we taste. Their stomachs are full of stitches and patches, like Harlequin.

COSTA

They swallow things, we chew. Their teeth are stuck to their jaws with glue. Their mouths are full of bridges, dams, dirt-roads, overpasses and freeways.

MICHELI

Did you know false teeth are tougher than real teeth? The other day I broke a tooth on a piece of nougat. My father said 'Here, I'll break a piece off for you, you're hopeless.' He just went crunch and broke it into a thousand pieces. He cracks nuts with his teeth. When he gets mad I'm terrified he's going to bite me. I'd probably get rabies.

LUCINI

Stop knocking your parents. I get on fine with my folks. If it wasn't for them I'd be on the bones of my ass.

RIPANDELLI

At least you've still got an ass. And you're a catholic. We had to hock our asses ages ago, right Costa?

COSTA

You bet. The way things are these days you can't run risks.

LUCINI

Continuing his discussion about his parents.

They're good, considerate people. They don't break my balls.

COSTA

I heard your mother was getting it on with the manager of the paper mill.

LUCINI

Bullshit. My mother's never been with any other man except my father. They've got a really strong relationship – they believe in sticking together.

COSTA

What a classic – everybody knows about it except you!

LUCINI

I'm warning you – I don't appreciate gossip and rumors about my mother.

RIPANDELLI

Would you prefer to hear something about your father?

LUCINI

Go to hell, Ripa, you're just a shit-stirrer. I'm not going to be your fall guy.

RIPANDELLI

Your old man launders dirty money. It's true.

LUCINI

Bullshit.

COSTA

It's common knowledge. The whole town knows.

RIPANDELLI

Haven't you ever wondered why he's always popping over to Switzerland, and why he's on the board of so many banks?

LUCINI

You slime. I refuse to even give you the satisfaction of seeing me lose my temper. Anyway, my father's my father and I'm me.

RIPANDELLI

Tautologies will get you nowhere, Lucini.

COSTA

You have to save up for your second childhood somehow. And your third, and your fourth. How else would our honourable fathers out there survive without their bribes, rake-offs and kickbacks?

RIPANDELLI

Where do you think those Mercedes parked outside come from?

COSTA

We're children of easy virtue – totally innocent and totally corrupt. Only you and your catholic ass try to hide from the unsavoury truth.

MICHELI

Leave the poor boy alone. If that's what he wants to believe, let him.

RIPANDELLI

Do you want us to drag your honourable old man through the mud too?

MICHELI

My father's a politician. Everybody slanders politicians – it goes with the territory.

COSTA

What did he give you for Christmas?

MICHELI

I don't owe him anything.

RIPANDELLI

How do you survive then, Micheli? You haven't got a job.

MICHELI

I write.

RIPANDELLI

He writes. What do you write? A secret diary?

MICHELI

I write whatever I feel like.

RIPANDELLI

He writes to ease the guilty conscience he's got about scrounging off his old man. And his mother gives him secret handouts.

COSTA

You're just as big a fool as the rest of us, Micheli.

MICHELI

Fool is a compliment, so thanks.

RIPANDELLI

Right, he's a fool among fools. A fool with a herringbone jacket, a gold bracelet, tweed trousers and a bank account. A well-bred fool – a good family man, a connoisseur of good food, an expert on flowers and wine ...

COSTA

A fool in the best tradition of fools.

MICHELI

Laughing.

Fool is fine – fools rush in, everybody's somebody's fool, now and then there's a fool such as I –

RIPANDELLI

Everybody loves a fool –

MICHELI

A son of fools and a father of fools –

RIPANDELLI

You mean you've got a kid, Micheli?

LUCINI

What a turn-up for the books!

RIPANDELLI

Not only do you believe in God, you've got a
secret drive to breed? You never cease to amaze
me.

MICHELI

You mean you've given up all hope of getting
married and having children?

RIPANDELLI

I've never suffered from such base instincts.

LUCINI

You were a kid once.

RIPANDELLI

Who told you that? I was born with a hairy chest, a three piece suit and specs on.

COSTA

You're a fool with a heart of gold, Lucini, but doesn't it wear a hole in your shirt?

LUCINI

Just because I've got some shreds of decency left, you don't have to give me such a hard time.

COSTA

We're giving him a hard time.

MICHELI

You're giving him a hard time.

COSTA

What a hard time we're having, giving Lucini a hard time!

RIPANDELLI

I bet you've even got a fiancée.

LUCINI

Sure I have. She's sixteen.

COSTA

And I bet she's a really nice girl.

LUCINI

Yeah. She is.

COSTA

And you probably don't ever fuck her, so she'll stay nice and pure for the wedding.

LUCINI

I don't know about that.

RIPANDELLI

So you're as corrupt as the rest of us – shame on you! A sixteen year old girl!

COSTA

He's never even introduced her to us. What a sleazebag – only sixteen!

MICHELI

And you want to have kids with this kid?

LUCINI

Why not? She's an orphan.

RIPANDELLI

She's an orphan. What better reason?

COSTA

Little orphan Annie!

MICHELI

Poor little mite!

LUCINI

Leave me alone, will you?

RIPANDELLI

Why should we? Didn't you know being left alone makes your balls shrivel up?

LUCINI

You're all piss and wind – crapping on, acting all cynical and superior. You're full of shit.

RIPANDELLI

We don't need you to tell us that. It all depends on how you handle the shit. You can still be right in the middle of the shit and not stink, as long as you keep on smoking classy cigarettes, thinking noble thoughts and laughing at everybody.

MICHELI

Come on, let's get back to the game. Whose deal is it?

LUCINI

Mine. Here, give me the cards.

RIPANDELLI

O.K., let's have a real fool's deal. We're playing for fool's gold.

COSTA

Deal those cards like a real bloodsucking scrounger.

Sniggers.

MICHELI

Notices the coats moving.

Hey, guys. We're being spied on.

RIPANDELLI

Looking Micheli in the eyes

What's the problem?

MICHELI

Look – those coats are moving.

They all turn around and see the coats moving.

RIPANDELLI

Must be God coming down to pass judgment on us.

COSTA

The old secondhand coat God.

RIPANDELLI

I can't see his rubber boots. Hey, that's a woman's foot! And it's barefoot! How about that!

A woman emerges from the coats.

LUCINI

It's the princess!

COSTA

Not God, just a goddess!

RIPANDELLI

Welcome aboard princess!

COSTA

You're just in time. We were starting to get bored.

MICHELI

What would've become of us if you hadn't appeared from under those coats, like Venus emerging from the sea?

347

PRINCESS

Oh. Good evening. I must have fallen asleep.

RIPANDELLI

Look at those beautiful arms. Like a swan.

PRINCESS

Me, a swan?

> *She looks at her flabby bare arms and laughs.*

A swan?

MICHELI

And look at those tiny feet. What size do you take? 45?

PRINCESS

Real duck's feet, eh?

> *Her voice sounds naive and child-like, but without affectation. She is cheerful and frank. She would appear pleasant but lost.*

When I was little I was always dressing up in my mother's high-heeled shoes, and staggering around the place. My feet must have grown to fit the shoes.

> *She laughs.*

MICHELI

They're not exactly Cinderella's size.

RIPANDELLI

Cinderella was just a little suburban girl with a castration complex. Any intelligent woman should have big feet. They're a mark of sincerity.

PRINCESS

Thank you!

> *She raises her coloured, stockinged feet and laughs.*

COSTA

> *In a grandiose, exaggerated manner, starting off a game which implicates the others*

What a beautiful body!

RIPANDELLI

> *Gleefully joining in the game.*

Princess. I do declare, here in front of everyone, the moment I saw you appear from that pile of coats, I fell in love with you. You stirred up something inside me, something I can't quite put my finger on. Will you come and dance with me?

PRINCESS

I'm sick of dancing out there. They're all over seventy, and all presidents, managers, councillors ... I drank five, no six, well maybe seven glasses of champagne, and then I must have fallen asleep. I can't remember exactly – is my dress very crumpled?

COSTA

Not at all. It's immaculate.

RIPANDELLI

Well, to tell the truth it is a bit creased. Why don't you take it off?

PRINCESS

You remind me of your father, young Ripandelli. He was a nice young man. You look like him a bit, but you're not as good looking as he was. You haven't got his impertinent nose, or his dreamy eyes that used to drive the girls crazy, or his moustache. Why don't you grow a moustache like your father's?

RIPANDELLI

For your information, princess, I am not my father's son. My mother gave birth to me by parthenogenesis, after she fell madly in love with herself when she was fifteen years old. The womb which bore me was as pure and immaculate as the Virgin Mary's.

PRINCESS

So you're a son of the holy ghost!

RIPANDELLI

More like a carrier pigeon. Sometimes I feel something pecking away in my brain, telling me to peck my way out of this pack of fools.

PRINCESS

You're a bit ordinary for a son of God. I know lots of young men like you – with their brains in their trousers. But I like you. You've got a good strong voice and nice eyes – almost as nice as your father's.

RIPANDELLI

Would you stop comparing me to my father? I'm no relation to him – by blood or by character.

PRINCESS

You're almost identical from the waist down. From what I can tell you're as well-hung as he is.

COSTA

Hey, I'm getting jealous. Why is Ripandelli getting all the attention? What about us?

MICHELI

We need some champagne for our new guest. I'll go and get some.

PRINCESS

Can you get something to eat while you're at it? I'm starving.

MICHELI

Right.

Micheli opens the glass doors. Laughter and dance music can be heard.

COSTA

Still having a wild time out there. Time those oldies got an early night.

RIPANDELLI

They've been dead for years so it wouldn't make much difference.

COSTA

You wouldn't still be hanging on for your inheritance if they were.

PRINCESS

Why shouldn't they enjoy themselves in their last years of life?

COSTA

That's what I said ten years ago. How presumptuous can you get?

PRINCESS

I could leave you an inheritance if I was dying, but I haven't got a cent.

RIPANDELLI

I don't want your money, princess. It's your body I want. What are the chances?

PRINCESS

I'm afraid my body's a bit dilapidated.

RIPANDELLI

Close to her. Softly.

I love you. You must believe me, princess. It might seem strange, but it's true. I only like older women. I know I'm perverted, but young girls make me want to throw up. I can't stand those freshly scrubbed, unwrinkled faces, and their stuck-up little noses and voices like angels'. They're so trusting and pleasant, and fresh and energetic – I can't bear that kind of peaches and cream puppy love. I love you, princess. It was love at first sight. Passionate love.

PRINCESS

These things happen. My niece went and fell in love with a man of sixty. And she's only twenty-one.

RIPANDELLI

Are you trying to cast aspersions on the originality of my perversion?

COSTA

It's different for men, princess. Men never fall in love with older women. They're incapable of it.

PRINCESS

He's just as fat and flabby and bald as the rest of them, and he's got false teeth too.

COSTA

The princess is giving you the cold shoulder, Ripandelli. You've got no chance.

RIPANDELLI

That's because she's intelligent. I love intelligent women. Don't you believe I love you, princess?

PRINCESS

I'd like to believe you. Perhaps you're like my niece.

LUCINI

Don't take any notice of them, they're putting you on. They're just playing games with you.

PRINCESS

I can play games too, you know.

COSTA

Some people even fall in love with dead people. Compared to them, an old man is like a three-year-old child.

PRINCESS

They must take them out of their coffins, caress them and possess them –

COSTA

Take who?

PRINCESS

Dead people.

COSTA

This princess has sure been around.

LUCINI

Signora, please –

PRINCESS

Signora? Why deprive me of a title that isn't mine to begin with? Didn't you know all the best princesses are make-believe ones, like the princess in the enchanted castle?

RIPANDELLI

Does that mean you love me?

PRINCESS

I don't know, Mr. Ripandelli. I don't know. I have to know somebody before I can love them. I hardly know you at all. I remember your father was a kind young man, but a bit cold. I think he loved me for a month or so, but that was all.

RIPANDELLI

I wish you'd stop bringing my father into this. I keep my snout well away from his troughs.

PRINCESS

Why? He's still a very handsome man.

RIPANDELLI

No particular reason. My chromosomes are different from his, that's all. Can I kiss you?

Micheli comes back with champagne and cakes.

MICHELI

Cakes and champagne!

PRINCESS

Taking a cake.

Delicious. Are there many left out there?

MICHELI

Cakes? No way – they've polished them all off. I had to track these down in the kitchen.

COSTA

Stop blathering and pour some champagne.

RIPANDELLI

Allow me, princess.

Pours her a glass of champagne.

PRINCESS

I've had too much already –

RIPANDELLI

I love loose women. Alcohol is a great aphrodisiac.

COSTA

Stop pussy-footing around, Ripa. I don't beat around the bush like him, princess. I'm more direct. I lust after you. Can I kiss your hand?

RIPANDELLI

Cut it out. This is between her and me. What right have you got to stick your nose into our affair?

COSTA

What right have you got to hog the game? We're playing too you know.

PRINCESS

Are you a pervert too, Mr. Costa? Don't you like girls either?

COSTA

I like a bit of everything, like Don Giovanni.

Singing.

'He usually praises / Blondes for their gentleness / Brunettes for their faithfulness / In white hair he finds sweetness / In winter he likes fat ones / In summer he likes thin ones / Tall ones impress him / Short ones beguile him / He makes conquests of old ones to add to his list'.

RIPANDELLI

What an insult. Stealing the woman I love, out of some perverse desire to make a conquest.

COSTA

I saw her first. I saw her under the coats.

RIPANDELLI

Oh no, you didn't. I did.

COSTA

I was blinded by love.

RIPANDELLI

And I was struck dumb. I'm still in a state of shock now.

PRINCESS

Please stop arguing. I like both of you.

RIPANDELLI

Oh no, you don't! You have to choose. It's him or me. There's no other solution.

PRINCESS

I can't choose. You're both very handsome young men.

MICHELI

Now you've offended me. What about me?

PRINCESS

You're all very handsome.

MICHELI

Well, they'll have to share with me. Why should I be the odd man out?

RIPANDELLI

Pour the princess some more champagne and stop gawking, you peasant!

LUCINI

This game of yours isn't funny at all, you know. You pigs.

RIPANDELLI

Pigs? Why pigs? I prefer hyenas – the lords of the jungle. Have you ever watched a hyena in action? More champagne, princess?

> *The princess sips champagne and laughs. She is amused by the game, and even though she realizes it could be dangerous, she is convinced she can survive unscathed. She sips and eats a cake.*

COSTA

What a lovely sight you are princess, all flushed with champagne, and slurring your speech like a little lost girl ... you really turn me on.

RIPANDELLI

What a blossom!

PRINCESS

A very wilted blossom. But sometimes age is no barrier to attraction, is it?

She knows very well this isn't true in their case, but she plays along with them openly.

RIPANDELLI

I love you passionately, princess. Oh God, those big sagging breasts! Let me kiss the tip of your nipple – just the tip!

PRINCESS

Let's pretend you just have. Isn't it so much better when you imagine things? Like wish fulfillment.

COSTA

That's too airy-fairy for me. I like to call a spade a spade.

RIPANDELLI

You've always been brilliant at ruining the atmosphere, Costa. You've got no sense of style.

COSTA

Fuck off, creep.

PRINCESS

Please, don't start fighting.

COSTA

You can't fancy that creep Ripandelli more than me? You've got to like me better than him, princess.

PRINCESS

I like you both. I wish I had two mouths to kiss you both at once.

RIPANDELLI

Yuck – fancy kissing him. I'd rather kiss myself. I spent my whole childhood kissing myself. Who's better looking – him or me?

PRINCESS

Looks aren't all that important. I like you both because you're nice and young – you're pleasure to look at. If my son was still alive he's be the same age as you.

COSTA

Don't speak of the dead, princess, you'll spoil everything. Your son's dead because he stuck a needle full of poison into his arm. That means he wanted to die. Let him rest in peace.

PRINCESS

Yes, may he rest in peace – he's in a better place. He got so violent towards the end. He used to shout and threaten me if I didn't give him money. Once he even tried to strangle me – I had his finger marks on my neck for a whole week. I sold everything for him – the house, the garden, my paintings, my jewels, the car ... He stripped me naked.

COSTA

We'd like to strip you naked too.

RIPANDELLI

I've been getting glimpses of those old, sagging breasts, they look so well-sucked by lovers and children, it's driving me mad. Show us your body. Please.

MICHELI

Starting with your breasts.

PRINCESS

When I was a girl I had lovely breasts, but now they're old and worn out.

RIPANDELLI

What do you mean? Your body's still young and luscious. Show us what you've got, princess.

MICHELI

Get'em off! Get'em off!

LUCINI

Leave the poor woman alone!

RIPANDELLI

He's just jealous – he wants to be in on the kissing too. Can he join in the game?

PRINCESS

Aren't you all friends?

LUCINI

Sure we're friends, but some of us have different tastes.

PRINCESS

Let me look at you.

Turning to Lucini.

Your forehead's so drawn. You look very melancholy.

LUCINI

Don't let those three animals take you for a ride.
Get out while the going's good.

PRINCESS

There's nothing to be afraid of. I was never a-
fraid of my son, either. I get on well with young
people.

COSTA

Will you look at this worm? Trying to get the
princess away from us like some snotty little
schoolboy?

RIPANDELLI

Let's make an ultimatum, shall we? If you haven't
got your clothes off in three minutes, we'll get
them off you. O.K?

PRINCESS

Why don't you take your clothes off? You've got
such nice bodies – I'd rather look at you.

COSTA

I see – a prick teaser!

365

RIPANDELLI

Take your clothes off, princess. Either do it of your own free will or we'll force you to. Take your pick.

PRINCESS

Why should I?

COSTA

Get'em off!

PRINCESS

Just a moment.

> *She has a moment of panic for the first time, but still thinks she has the situation under control.*

I'll do it.

> *She starts unbuttoning her dress, but more to humour them than to take it off, which she has no intention of doing.*

I must have had a lot to drink ... I can see all these faces, laughing at me, but not laughing properly, more like somebody with a belly-ache ... My son used to make faces like that ... when he's started breaking something but wasn't sure whether he should go the whole way ... He was sorry about breaking it because he knew it would upset me, but he couldn't resist smashing the whole thing to pieces ...

COSTA

Stop gibbering, you old bag!

He grabs her arm and rips her dress off in one movement. She stands there in her underclothes, a comical sight, all wrapped up in vests and woolen tights.

PRINCESS

Stop that. I told you I'd do it. I'm perfectly capable of doing it myself.

She pretends to strip again.

What a pity you've changed your tone of voice. It was so much fun before, playing this little game, but now you've changed your tone. My son used to do that when I didn't give him the money he was after. His voice sounded like it came from right down in his stomach, like some poison that was giving him indigestion. It sounded all deep and strangled, and suddenly I couldn't even recognize it, it was so mean and nasty.

RIPANDELLI

Shut up, will you?

MICHELI

Cut the crap, princess. What a pain in the ass!

Ripandelli goes up to her and throws the contents of his glass in her face. For a moment she is horrified, and then makes another attempt to calm herself down by talking.

PRINCESS

What did you do that for, young Ripandelli? Your father would never have done a thing like that. Right to the very end, right to the very end he always kissed me tenderly ... then he went away ... He'd fallen for another woman, the wife of one of his friends, but he never treated me badly ... He used to adore me, never said a bad word about me ... I remember one time he came to see me, and when I opened the door, his face was all hidden behind a big bunch of flowers ... all I could see was the tips of his moustache. So I told him –

She is interrupted by Costa, who tears off her necklace in a rage.

COSTA

Get this crap off!

Ripandelli joins in and tears off her petti-coat. But she has another garment under-neath, and another — like poor people who live in cold houses wear layers of garments, all of the same poor quality.

PRINCESS

Stop it! Stop it! Let me go!

She goes towards the door.

COSTA

Quick, grab her before she gets away!

Micheli grabs her from behind and holds her while Ripandelli keeps on tearing away at her clothes. Lucini is the only one who does not join in. He stays sitting on a chair, watching them disapprovingly.

RIPANDELLI

Trying to get away, eh? And where do you think you're going?

PRINCESS

What do you want from me?

COSTA

Nothing.

RIPANDELLI

We want you to take your clothes off – and hurry up about it.

COSTA

Get these rags off.

> *Costa starts pulling at her clothes, but every time he takes off a garment there is another one underneath. He becomes visibly annoyed.*

PRINCESS

Leave me alone! What do you want from me?

COSTA

Nothing.

RIPANDELLI

What do you think we want from you? Nothing!

MICHELI

Absolutely nothing.

> *Laughing.*

COSTA

Absolutely nothing at all.

While Costa and Micheli hold her, Ripandelli leaps on top of her and is about to rape her standing up. She struggles and breaks away with one last effort and lurches towards the door, beating on it with her fists.

PRINCESS

Help me!

Ripandelli, infuriated, grabs the champagne bottle and smashes it over her head. She falls to the floor on her back. The three men stare at her in amazement.

RIPANDELLI

Almost as if seeing her for the first time

You see that mole?

COSTA

What mole?

RIPANDELLI

That mole on her neck.

COSTA

What bloody mole? You've killed her, you idiot!

MICHELI

Maybe she's just passed out. Let's try and wake her up.

Micheli bends over her, and tries to lift her up, but she flops back, all her limbs inert. He places his ear on her chest and then shakes his head.

MICHELI

She's dead.

COSTA

Cover her up.

RIPANDELLI

You cover her up.

LUCINI

Going up to her.

You've killed her, you bloody murderers! I knew this would happen!

COSTA

You were part of it.

LUCINI

I was sitting over there by the window. You're all witnesses.

MICHELI

Do you think the judge will let you off just because you were sitting over by the window?

COSTA

You're worse than we are, Lucini. You sat and watched the whole thing and never even lifted a finger.

MICHELI

We're all accomplices whether you like it or not.

RIPANDELLI

Just keep on blabbing away about it, you fucking idiots. Someone'll come in any minute now and we can tell them all about it.

LUCINI

We'll all be charged with murder. Oh God.

Covers his face with his hands.

COSTA

Stop you whining, dickhead, and use your head. The princess lived alone, right, so no one's going to notice she's not around for a week or so. So let's just carry on with our poker game, and leave her under the sofa. When everybody's gone home, we'll go and dump her in the river.

MICHELI

And everyone'll think it was suicide. A poor old woman, living on her own – it's logical enough.

LUCINI

What if anybody asks where she is?

COSTA

Why should they? And how would we know? We can just say we haven't seen her.

LUCINI

You can get rid of her by yourself. I'm not going to dump that poor old woman in the river. You killed her, you dump her.

MICHELI

You were in on raping her, weren't you? Or at least on watching her getting raped, which is worse.

LUCINI

Bullshit. I told you to leave her alone right from the start. I've got nothing to do with it.

RIPANDELLI

That mole.

MICHELI

To Lucini.

You were here. We all saw you grab her. We're all witnesses.

RIPANDELLI

That mole – how come it's so black?

COSTA

You and your bloody mole.

RIPANDELLI

It's like it's staring at me.

COSTA

Go to hell, Ripa!

RIPANDELLI

It is staring at me.

COSTA

Give us a hand to drag her under the sofa.

LUCINI

I'm not involved. I'm not involved.

COSTA

Come on, you fool.

MICHELI

To Lucini.

If you don't hurry up we'll say you did it.

> *Lucini decides to help the others. The four of them put the woman under the sofa, although Ripandelli is still distracted by the mole which is staring at him.*

COSTA

Now back to the card table.

> *The others do as he says automatically. Costa picks up the cards and shuffles them, eyeing the others. Then he deals.*

COSTA

One, two, three, four, five ... Who's going to open the bidding?

> *To Ripandelli.*

How about you?

RIPANDELLI

No.

COSTA

To Micheli.

You?

MICHELI

O.K. Two hundred.

COSTA

Got a good hand, eh?

LUCINI

I'm not involved.

COSTA

What a bloody spoilsport. Here's four cards. That should keep you in the game.

To Ripandelli.

How many for you?

RIPANDELLI

Three.

COSTA

One, two, three. And one for myself.

MICHELI

I can never get a decent run.

COSTA

They're easier to get when they're queen high.

MICHELI

So who's going to see me for two hundred?

COSTA

I will.

RIPANDELLI

Visibly returning to normal.

Me too.

COSTA

To Lucini.

How about you?

BLACKOUT

AGMV
MARQUIS
Québec, Canada
1998